Irish History

*A Concise Overview of the History
of Ireland From Start to End*

Eric Brown

Legal & Disclaimer

The information contained in this book and its contents is not designed to replace or take the place of any form of medical or professional advice; and is not meant to replace the need for independent medical, financial, legal or other professional advice or services, as may be required. The content and information in this book has been provided for educational and entertainment purposes only.

The content and information contained in this book has been compiled from sources deemed reliable, and it is accurate to the best of the Author's knowledge, information, and belief. However, the Author cannot guarantee its accuracy and validity and cannot be held liable for any errors and/or omissions. Further, changes are periodically made to this book as and when needed. Where appropriate and/or necessary, you must consult a professional (including but not limited to your doctor, attorney, financial advisor or such other professional advisor) before using any of the suggested remedies, techniques, or information in this book.

Upon using the contents and information contained in this book, you agree to hold harmless the Author from and against any damages, costs, and expenses, including any legal fees potentially resulting from the application of any of the information provided by this book. This disclaimer applies to any loss, damages or injury caused by the use and application, whether directly or indirectly, of any advice or information presented, whether for breach of contract, tort, negligence, personal injury, criminal intent, or under any other cause of action.

You agree to accept all risks of using the information presented inside this book.

You agree that by continuing to read this book, where appropriate and/or necessary, you shall consult a professional (including but not limited to your doctor, attorney, or financial advisor or such other advisor as needed) before using any of the suggested remedies, techniques, or information in this book.

Table of Contents

Introduction

Just like any history, the history of Ireland seems an endless series of struggles and bloody battles as the local natives fight against invading foreign forces. Often perceived as a remote, distant, and isolated backwater, the Irish history denies any truth of it even when it is often discussed merely as an offshoot to that of the English.

Ireland has its own distinctive character as exemplified by its history. Ireland close connection with Britain somehow has had profound influences on the country in many ways although the influence in culture managed to flow in both ways and yet remained to be just one portion of the adverse and fascinating history.

The country's history is embedded not just in the cityscapes but scattered throughout the numerous landscape and throughout the country in the form of historical monuments and archaeological edifice. A closer look at the landscape itself reveals the historical imprints that account for what Ireland is today.

Those long years of hostility and tumultuous battles with the colonists had helped engraved in every Irish their own national identity which have been long trampled by foreign invaders and which today have to mold them to appreciate their freedom.

This book "The Irish History" is written to make everyone aware of how Ireland had gone through those periods of hostility and colonization despite the power struggle between religion and politics which lead to loss of lives and properties of the common people, still, they fought both for survival and for redemption of their lands which have been stolen in broad daylight.

The History of Ireland is a challenge to everyone, especially to those descendants of the people who have fought hard so that they can take back their lands for their children and future generations. Many generations have passed since the last Civil War, but the lesson of the

War is enough to make everyone aware through this book that power struggle can occur anytime and unless you unify and get ready to protect your lands, there will always be invaders to come and take it from you.

Nationality is not only seen in arms struggles but in the unification of your dreams and hopes for a better future of the lands that have been your home and that of your forefathers who have willingly sacrificed their lives for the freedom of the next generations.

Chapter 1: Ireland in the Early Time

The topography of Ireland as we can see today was actually made up of waves after waves of glaciers a long time ago and before the coming of settlers. But underneath those covering sheets of glaciers, Ireland was made up of very old rock.

During the mountain-building era – the Caledonian orogeny and Armorican phase, a large portion of north-western Europe were folded to form the mountains of Himalayas. The long period covering the Ice Ages reduced these mountains with the remnant of the once vast mountain chains discovered in Scotland, Scandinavia, and Ireland. About 75% of the land area of Ireland today is below 492 feet while the highest point is about 3,414 high which is the Carrantoohill, County Kerry.

The majority of the regions of Ireland were formed by glaciation in the last period of the Ice Age of 20,000-10,000 years ago which retained deposits of sheets of drift material in lowland areas. Such material later formed the unevenly laid fertile agricultural land consisting of gravel and clay. The shape of the material varies across the province. Its undulating form around Dublin makes the land great for farming while in central lowlands; the material was formed with an extremely irregular surface. Lakes were formed in the hollows which later turned into quagmires which are a distinguishing characteristic of the region today.

The ice melted last to the north of the central plain where it molded the landscape into countless numbers of tightly-packed elongated, teardrop-shaped hills of sand, gravel, and rock-forming other moving glacier ice. These drumlins, as they are called extend from Donegal Bay in the west to Strangford Lough in the east which are not conducive for agricultural farming and tend to produce a natural barrier to settlement throughout the history of Ireland.

Areas in the upland were stripped bare of soil by the ice which has become one of the sources of the drift material scattered across the lowlands. Ice that once covered the mountain-side valleys formed greatly curved basins referred to as "corries."

During the next 2000 years, the formation of the ice slowed down until only the Ulster remained under the sheet of ice. The rising sea level brought a flood to the lower lands, but a land bridge still manages to connect the southeastern tip of Ireland to the southwestern portion of England. The Irish Sea which was trapped between the ice sheet in the north and the land bridge formed a vast freshwater lake. At this point in time, the first plant appeared to reclaim the rocky wilderness that formed Ireland Britain. Grass began to cover the land, and Juniper trees started to grow. Using the land bridge, many wild animals including the Giant Deer wandered off into Ireland [1].

Low-land areas surrounding Ireland, Britain, and Europe were gradually flooded as the sea level rose to overwhelm the land bridge and filling up the freshwater lake with salt water. After the flood, the land bridge still showed up on many occasions. The vast Dogger Bank lying between Britain and Denmark was entirely submerged in water, and today it lies 50,165 feet below the North Sea when 10,000 years ago, it was covered by a great rain forest.

With the melting of the ice, rivers and lakes were formed in the landforms left behind by glaciers. The new river pattern in Ireland was entirely different from those previous ones making it difficult for us to imagine what Ireland looked like in the ice age and also because the previous landscape was completely destroyed.

Even with its destruction, the Ice Ages were able to leave behind a beautiful topography that played a significant role in the unfolding history of Ireland. The first humans are thought to have first set foot in Ireland 9000 years ago or during 7000 B.C. Although people have made some alterations on the landscape, still, it could not contest the great changes that the Ice Age had once brought.

Mesolithic Ireland

Recorded to be one of the last places in Europe to be discovered and settled by humans, the first humans who settled in Mesolithic Ireland [2] originally came from Scotland. It was said that they traveled here using boats and settled at the place known nowadays as Antrim County around 8000 B.C. It is believed that, during that time, momentary land bridges reappeared from the Irish Sea and Northern Scotland due to rising land and levels, allowing both human and animal migration in this place. Compared to other European countries, the human presence here is believed to be only about 10,000 years old.

The early humans in these parts are known to be fishermen, concentrating their search for food on seashores, lakes, rivers, and waterways. These early residents rarely venture inside the forest, leaving Ireland's forest ecosystem untouched and unaffected.

The earliest recorded Mesolithic activity in Ireland is found in Antrim, the country's only source of flint as well as in Sligo and Londonderry. Archaeologists also found charcoal and Mesolithic hut remains in Mount Sandel and have said to be dated between 7000 and 6500 B.C. In addition to that, they also found thousands of flint tools in The Curran, a place near Larne in Antrim and pieces of evidence of Mesolithic settlement in Lough Boora, thereby proving concrete evidence of Mesolithic activity in the country.

Around 4000 B.C., near the end of Mesolithic Era, the settlers started copying coiled pottery technology from more advanced Neolithic tribes from Eastern Europe. However, unlike in France, these 'Mesolithic Irishmen' did not leave any earthworks even though they have the knowledge to make pottery as well as in building huts and making tools. It is said that the earliest earthenwares discovered in

Ireland are Neolithic.

In the last part of Mesolithic Era, Ireland's climate became wetter, turning lakes in the western part to bogs. Because of this, the land was unable to sustain or support the entire population, either resulting in settlers migrating to other nearby European countries or death due to starvation.

Mesolithic Ireland Life

Life in Mesolithic Ireland consists of flint, skin huts, a meat-rich diet with fruits and nuts on the side, and a nomadic way of living. Just like in any other starting lives in Europe, people of Mesolithic Ireland consist of hunters and gatherers. Using their flint harpoons, they primarily spear and eat fish during the early stages of settlement and lived near rivers and lakes inside skin huts. As the fish supply in water areas dwindled, they then moved inside the forested areas where they hunt birds and game as well as gathered fruits, berries and nuts. The skin covering used in their huts proved to be useful since they can just bring it wherever they go. It is recorded, however, that they just venture inside the forested areas but set up their camps near waterways, most probably to ensure a safe and stable water supply as well as fish.

Hunters mainly look for deer and wild boar inside forested areas for food as well as their skins, which were used either to make clothing, repair the skin canvass in their huts or to make new ones.

The discovery and practice of Farming are what first signaled the Neolithic Age. Not only did this practice provide the people with food, giving them another handy option besides hunting, gathering, and fishing; but it also gives rise to the concept of building bigger and permanent homes until eventually, communities. Needless to say, farming gave the people time to invent more useful things, improve the existing ones and innovate their technology. [4]

It's sad to know, however, that it is not the Mesolithic people in Ireland who suddenly 'discovered' and practiced farming during their time. Instead, this was practiced by the Neolithic settlers from Britain, who came to Ireland and drove the Mesolithic people away from their territory. Shreds of evidence found from Cashelkeelty in Kerry suggest that farming started in the country from 3900 to 3000 B.C.

In order to build their permanent farms, these Neolithic settlers started farming by clearing out upland forests either by using their stone axes or by burning it. Ireland doesn't have lots of native cereal crops, so these settlers brought wheat and barley to plant in their farms. And since wild pigs are the only animals here that can be potentially raised as livestock, the settlers also brought cows, goats, and sheep along with them.

The Neolithic settlers' plan worked at first. However, as time passed, erosion and overgrazing in the newly-cleared uplands resulted in acidification, eventually turning those into peat bogs that are unable to sustain plant life. In other words, most of Ireland's upland peat bogs are primarily caused by Neolithic settlers' farming practice and not just the climate.

In addition to farming, Neolithic settlers also utilized Porcellanite technology. Tougher than flint used by Mesolithic people, Porcellanite was used in their axes, knives and other tools. This rock enabled them to clear larger trees in the upland forests faster than using flint tools. And unlike flint, which is supplied only in Antrim, porcellanite was also mined here as well as in Cushendall and Rathlin. Archaeologists found porcellanite axes not only in Ulster but also in other parts of Ireland, extending up to Southern England. This evidence suggests that the Neolithic Irish settlers are trading with Neolithic Britons as well as exchanging knowledge and technologies with them.

Neolithic Ireland Life

Compared to Mesolithic Irish, archaeological evidence suggests that Neolithic Irish settlers lived in larger and permanent houses as well as having larger communities. Pieces of evidence found in Ceide Fields in Mayo county that Neolithic Irish communities may have farmed large tracts of upland. And since they practically stay in one place, Neolithic Irish settlers build their houses from materials such as tree trunks and mud-covered woven branches they obtained from clearing upland forests. In addition to that, they may have also made large multi-purpose buildings in the center of each community.

It can be safely assumed that a Neolithic settler lived in a wattle-and-daub house and was a part of a community consisting of at least thirty people living together. At first, they occupied the uplands since it is easier to clear away compared to lowlands, making it ready for both farming and habitation. The materials obtained from the trees have been used for many things, primarily for building houses and fuel. Field boundaries were later set up by building stone walls.

In addition to farming, Neolithic settlers [3] also raised sheep, cows, goats, which they brought along with them, and wild pigs, which are abundant in the area. Though being small at first, a Neolithic community gave rise to other communities until eventually; these communities formed a tribe, establishing trade relations to one another.

When it comes to cooking food, Neolithic Irish cooked their food and lit their fires indoors, as suggested by the small hole in the roof of their houses, allowing the smoke to escape.

The third remarkable invention that the Neolithic Irish used in this era is none other than Pottery itself. According to archaeological pieces of evidence found throughout Ireland, the settlers made their own pots by coiling long pieces of wet clay round and round and building a basic-shaped pot before smoothing it down. 'Customized pots' are decorated either by pressing twigs, stones or fingers when the clay is still wet before baking it in a hot fire.

Depending on its size, these pots are either used as oil lamps, in cooking as well as in storing food and water. Decorations in customized pots do not only improve a pot's individual look; it may also have served as identification of some sort to its owner.

It is still uncertain when it comes to the topic of how the Neolithic people bury their dead. Archaeological evidence found in one place suggests that cremation of the deceased is common. In another place, however, human bones are also found, suggesting that entombment of the deceased is also practiced. Given this situation, it can be assumed that religious beliefs and traditions in a particular tribe or community had influenced Neolithic people on how they bury their own dead.

As the population in the uplands increased, the farming practices of the Neolithic people, as well as overgrazing of their livestock, resulted to the entire land becoming peat bogs, making it acidic and unable to support vegetation. Because of this, exploration and settlement started in the lowlands.

Chapter 2: The Bronze Age to Iron Age

While the Bronze Age in Ireland is coming to an end, Celtic Influence spread almost throughout Europe. This influence (not an empire) started in the Alps in Central Europe before spreading to Iberian Peninsula (modern-day Spain and Portugal), Gaul (modern-day France), Teuton (modern-day Germany), Balkans and even Turkey. During that time, the well-known Roman Empire is just starting, practically ignoring the territories beside them. It was also during that time that Ireland and Britain were known to the Celts as Pretanic Islands.

The discovery and utilization of metals became the signal of a new age. A key event in human history, metals is nonetheless the first materials that can be mined, melted and molded into any desired shape. It can also be molded and crafted into useful things such as tools and utensils or decorations for both humans and their home. And last but not the least, it can also be made into stronger and tougher weapons that are way deadlier than those made with wood and stone. However, compared to other European countries, the Bronze Age started in Ireland two thousand years later.

Around 2000 B.C., settlers from France traveled to Ireland, most probably by boats, and shared the knowledge of bronze-working with the Neolithic Irish, which signaled the arrival of the country's Bronze Age. Having relatively large copper deposits, production of bronze, an alloy of copper and tin, became possible throughout Ireland. However, copper is found only in locations that are actually devoid of any human activity during the Mesolithic and Neolithic Age. Because of this, those who learned metalworking left their respective communities and started their new life in copper-rich locations such as Western Munster, Cork and Kerry counties. [5]

Mining Copper, one of the two key elements in making bronze, is somewhat dangerous if done carelessly. According to evidence found inside Mount Gabriel in Cork County, the copper ore was possibly extracted by lighting fires inside the mine and, as the walls become hot, it will then be doused with water so that their tools could easily remove the ore. Aside from the risk of the entire wall breaking down, dangerous gases can also be found inside the mines, gases that are mostly flammable and poisonous by nature.

On the other hand, there isn't much tin to mine inside Ireland, probably giving the possibility of the country importing their much-needed tin from the place that is now known as England.

During that time, what is copper made into?

Since tools are the main requirement even after the Neolithic Age, copper was usually crafted into tools such as axes, picks, and other farming implements. Cooking and eating etiquette is also evolving slowly during that time, giving rise to crafting of kitchen knives, cauldrons, bowls, and platters. And most of all, weapons specifically made to kill wild animals as well as human beings became popular, marking its increase in manufacture. Needless to say, these weapons also gave rise to various conflicts and wars against opposing communities and tribes during that time.

Aside from Bronze, the Bronze Age also signaled the discovery and first use of gold. Known for being useless when it comes to crafting tools and such, gold became a highly desirable material when it comes to making ornaments and other decorations because of its color and rarity. Since it is very valuable, its possession and usage may have given rise to the separation between rich and poor classes in the society, if not aristocracy. Because of this coincidence, that period in the Bronze Age somewhat became the 'First Golden Age' in Ireland.

Bronze Age Ireland Life

Even though that some pieces of evidence found from Carrigillihy in Cork county suggest the existence of stone houses during this time, most people in this age still lived in wattle-and-daub houses. The only noticeable improvement when it comes to housing is the usage of circular wooden fences that serve as a boundary of some sort as well as additional security.

Cooking methods also improved because of Fulacht Fian, the cooking place for Bronze Age people. A wood-lined trough dug from the ground, and the fulacht fian was filled with water before putting a heated stone in. When the eater inside it boils, large chunks of meat are added. A very common sight in southwest Ireland, fulacht fian is being used until 1600 A.D. According to Geoffrey Keating, these things are also used for boiling water.

The discovery of metal also improved Bronze Age agriculture. Compared to porcellanite of the Neolithic age, tools and other farming implements made from bronze are more reliable and don't easily wear out. In addition to that, bronze tools can be sharpened and melted again if broken.

It's also a sad thing to know that this age also signaled mankind's first use of weapons that were specifically designed to kill other humans. Because of the growing population, food supply became a problem, giving rise to disputes between various communities. Eventually, the disputes left unsettled by words alone resulted in armed conflict, leading to the demand for weapons made to defend oneself as well as kill enemies.

The Arrival of the Celts and Iron Age

While the Bronze Age in Ireland is coming to an end, Celtic Influence spread almost throughout Europe. This influence (not an empire) started in the Alps in Central Europe before spreading to Iberian Peninsula (modern-day Spain and Portugal), Gaul (modern-day France), Teuton (modern-day Germany), Balkans and even Turkey. During that time, the well-known Roman Empire is just starting, practically ignoring the territories beside them. It was also during that time that Ireland and Britain were known to the Celts as Pretanic Islands.

As the Celtic influence arrived in Ireland and Britain in year 500 B.C., the Celts also brought Iron and the knowledge of its use along with them. Compared to bronze, iron is stronger and more durable. However, it also requires more heat as well as effort and skill to work with, limiting its use to making tools as well as weaponry. It is the reason why bronze objects are still widely-used during that age.

It is still uncertain as to how Celtic Influence really arrived in Ireland. For some historians, Celts used their knowledge of Iron as well as numbers to spread their influence, effectively erasing any existing culture from Bronze Age. Others said that those Celts actually came from the Iberian Peninsula who escaped the Roman Empire, finally settling in Pretanic Islands. Still, others said that the Hallstatt group of Celts arrived before the end of the Bronze Age and started to spread their influence but failed to make it effective throughout the country. However, their influence was later supported by the La Tene cultural group, who arrived in Ireland after 300 B.C.

Though being regarded as pseudo-historical, the earliest records that we have about Celtic Ireland are from Greek, Carthaginian, and Roman writers who probably got their story from sailors who ventured in the British Isles. In 4th Century A.D., the Roman writer Avienus called Ireland in his writings Insula Sacra (Holy Island) and its people gens hiernorum, which were thought to be a Latinization, Ierne (Greek word for Ireland). The Greek writer Pytheas called the British Isles Pretanic Islands, which came from the Celtic word Priteni. And in year 52 B.C., Romans started calling Ireland Hibernia, which is probably extracted again from Ierne.

The most interesting record of Ireland's historical account is that of Greek writer Ptolemy. Published in his book Geographic, his map of Ireland was based on an account from year 100 A.D. but compiled in the second century A.D. It is sad, however, that there are no surviving originals in existence nowadays. The only copy remaining is dated from the year 1490 A.D. This map of Ptolemy enabled the historians to identify and name some of the Celtic tribes in Ireland during that time. Many of these tribe names have been badly corrupted by being passed via word-of-mouth, and most of them are unidentifiable with known tribes. The map also contains names of rivers as well as islands that can be identified nowadays.

Celtic Ireland Life

Even if the Celtic Culture managed to influence almost all Europe, part of Celtic Ireland's culture is still under Bronze Age influence. This cultural influence can be seen in their Heroic Tales such as the Ulster Cycle. Doubted by most historians at first, these tales describe the way of life of Celts during that time. Even if the description of events is somewhat exaggerated and may have undergone various revisions, the stories accurately describe the way of life in Celtic Ireland.

A culture mainly based around war, Celtic Ireland is believed to be divided into dozens, if not hundreds, of small and petty kingdoms. In each Kingdom, druids, poets, and blacksmiths are respected greatly; Druids for their soothsaying and prophecies, Blacksmiths for their skill in crafting tools and weapons of war and Poets for recording and putting the achievements and exploits of their warriors to verse, their heroism being sung in every important event.

It is also recorded that competition for the 'hero's portion' is done during the celebratory banquet after every victorious battle. The victor after the challenge will not just have the food prepared to fit the hero; he will also have the 'bragging rights' up until the next battle.

Political Structure

The aristocracy during this time is determined through individual strength and valor. In other words, a warrior who wants to become the next king should prove himself worthy in every battle while staying alive. Needless to say, it is expected that he should bring home the head of their enemy king or commander after the battle.

Unless the former king dies, the strongest and most valorous warrior will be given the privilege to take part in a 'Rite of Combat' against their own king. Depending on the conditions set beforehand, the loser will either be put to death or banished out of their kingdom.

At the time of the late Celtic Period, the country is believed to have been divided into two hundred small kingdoms or less (Tuath), each ruled by a king. Depending on their individual power, a king can be either classified to one of these three existing ruler grades during that time: Ri Tuaithe, Ruiri or Ri Ruirech. Ri Tuaithe rules over a single kingdom or territory. A Ruiri or Great King, on the other hand, is an overlord who either had an allegiance of or overseeing a number of other kings. A Ri Ruirech or King of Overkings (overlords) is the most influential, ruling an entire province. Because of the Ri Ruirech's sphere of influence, the whole country is divided into at least ten warring provinces during that time, until it eventually settled into four different provinces (Connaught, Ulster, Munster, and Leinster) as of today. The royal sites, however, remains intact in most of the displaced provinces.

As for the common folk, life means living inside wattle-and-daub houses and farms protected by a circular enclosure. Most of these farms have access to higher grounds where their animals graze. Almost every farmer plant grain crops and practice dairying. And since most farms are self-sustained, most of them don't need to trade just for food. The only problem for the common folk during this time is the passing-through warriors as well as invaders, who raid livestock as well as burn and pillage their farms. It is believed that there are at least a million people living in Ireland by year 400 A.D. However, their numbers decreased because they were affected by the recurring famine and plague, which had found its way to Europe during that time.

Chapter 3: The Advent of Christianity

The early Christian era occurs between 400 A.D. – 800 A.D. The first Christians to travel to Ireland probably came from Gaul (France) and Britain. There are no historical records showing how the Early Christian Era began in Ireland. However, historical records began to be recorded when the monastic settled in and started making manuscripts.

Pre-Christian Ireland Irish people are practicing druidism before Christianity was introduced in Ireland. They built many ritual sites like the Passage Tomb of Newgrange that was built in ancient Ireland during the Stone Age.

As a symbol of the importance of their beliefs and sun worship, the druids erected many monuments throughout Ireland.

Christian Missionaries in Ireland

Many people believed that Palladius was the first to introduce and establish Christianity in Ireland for he was the first canonical bishop to Ireland. This led to the belief that the first Christians to settle in the land of the Irish were the four "Palladian Bishops", namely:

- St. Ailbe of Emly
- St. Abban of Moyarny
- St. Ciaran of Saigir
- St. Declan of Ardmore

These four settled in Munster or southern part of Ireland.

Palladius' Arrival

When St. Palladius set sail for Ireland, he arrived at Hy-Garchon (today's Wicklow) on 431 A.D. unfortunately, he stayed there for a very short period of time. He was banished by the denizens of Hy-

Garchon off their lands. So, he left and sailed to the Orkney Islands in Scotland. He never set foot again in Ireland.

St. Patrick's Arrival

Though there is no exact date to tell of St. Patrick's arrival in Ireland, he was believed to have settled there around 432 A.D. St. Patrick was enslaved in Ireland. He escaped and returned to Britain, his home and then became a cleric. Later, he returned as a Christian Missionary in the northern and western part of Ireland.

St. Patrick came to a small island off the coast of Skerries coast (now known as Inish- Patrick) wherein near this location; he converted Benignus, a son of an Irish chieftain. Until the Vikings invaded the land, it is believed that the monastery that St. Patrick founded flourished on the island.

St. Patrick also converted a local pagan chieftain named Dichu mac Trichim in Saul (modern-day County Down) who then donated a barn in return. This barn was later converted to a church and served as a gift to St. Patrick.

In the next 30 years, St. Patrick continued his life as a Christian missionary in Ireland. He converted many pagans, local chieftains into Christianity and established worship places.

From Pagans to Christians

Though Palladius mission to Ireland seemed unsuccessful, on the other hand, St. Patrick's became fruitful. People may seem to perceive St. Patrick as a pirate or a warrior and grew weary of his appearances at first, but later they noticed his gentle approach. This act gave them little reluctance to be baptized and be converted to Christianity. To convert native Irish pagans to Christians, St. Patrick may have used different illustrations.

The shamrock is one of those famous illustrations that most people believed St. Patrick used to teach trinity to his followers. He also used some familiar things to the pagans for his illustrations. There were also some important figures that were popularized by Christianity in Ireland. They were St. Finnian of Clonnard, St. Brigid of Kildare, St. Brendan, St. Enda and Columcille.

Christianity in Ireland's History

Christianity played a major role in Irish history and society. As Christianity flourished, monasteries were built all over Ireland. Languages, literature, and art taught by the disciples gathered popularity throughout Europe. Because of this, not only scholars were attracted to Ireland but invited Viking raids as well.

After the Anglo-Normans Invasion, the English became involved in Irish affairs by the 12th century. New laws were instituted that oppressed the Irish Catholics. As ordered by The Crown of Ireland Act 1542, all monasteries in Ireland were forced to shut down.

In 1649, prior to Oliver Cromwell's invasion, many places of worship were removed. To remove Irish people from land ownership, the Cromwellian Act of Settlement 1652 was proclaimed, and in 1655, the Cromwellian Act of Settlement was altered by The Act of Explanation that enforces the return of one-third of the land by the Cromwellian settlers as compensation to the Catholics.

After 4 years, Oliver Plunkett was appointed by Rome as the Archbishop of Armagh. He then began a programme that reorganized structures and revived the Church which was almost destroyed in Ireland.

More Penal Laws were passed in 1673 together with the Test Act that commands the institution of the Holy Communion to be taken in the Anglican Church's manner by the clergy and laymen. This Act was refused by Oliver Plunkett that led to his arrest in 1679. He was charged with treason and executed in London on July 1, 1681. Since then, Oliver Plunkett was considered an Irish martyr and became a celebrated saint.

More anti-Catholic penal laws that outlawed the Catholic clergy were introduced after the Flight of the Wild Geese in 1691 and when William of Orange conquered Ireland. The state of affairs in Ireland became severe with poverty when it landed in the hands of non-Catholics in the 19th century. When Daniel O'Connell founded the Catholic Association in 1823, he succeeded in peacefully fighting for full emancipation. But in the latter part of the century, the land fight becomes violent resulting in land wars.

Christianity in Ireland Today

As of 2011 Census in Ireland, Christianity still remains as the predominant religion of the country. Majority or 84% of the Irish population is Catholic, and The Church of Ireland ranks next. Still, Christianity is taught and practiced in schools and many families remain as devoted followers of the church

Chapter 4: Ireland in the Middle Ages

Medieval Ireland

Early medieval Ireland (800 A.D.-1166) was a well-settled, prosperous, rural country that has a very tumultuous history. It was famous for its monasteries not only because these serve as centers for religion and education, but Irish monasteries were also places of great wealth and commerce. Ireland became an irresistible attraction for Vikings and raiders that left ineradicable marks in their history and country.

Ireland was divided into tuathas or small kingdoms. There were about 80-100 tuathas. Each kingdom has an Oenach (local assembly) composed of professionals, landowners, and craftsmen. The Oenach's function was the following:

- Create policies
- Declare war or peace on other groups or tuathas
- Elect or dispose of their king

The territory of Irish kings was owned by all freemen of their kingdoms. But still, the subjects owe their kings (the Uí Néill's were one of the few powerful kings that reigned over these groups) military services and taxes. For reasons that benefit everyone, the Tuatha becomes united. Though in-fighting existed among families at times when they have comes to select a new king, all in all, life was good in Ireland.

Tuatha kings, poets, and clergies were considered sacred in Ireland. They don't have to do manual work. Basically, Gaelic society was a case system that starts from landowners that were freemen down to those that don't have lands. Laws of the organization were specific and written between 600-900 A.D. in the Brehon Laws.

The Age of the Vikings

Vikings are a group of people who lived in Northern Europe, especially in areas known nowadays as Denmark and Norway. Also known as Norsemen, Ostmen, and Nords, Vikings are warriors known for their ferocity as well as valor in battle.

Because of political pressure in Scandinavia (the collective name for Denmark, Sweden, and Norway) during that time, nobles, as well as royals of various provinces, were forced to find territories of their own elsewhere. Most of these are younger sons who had failed to inherit any estate that their father owned. Along with their trusted band of fellow warriors, these men began to travel westward, raiding and pillaging nearby settlements. They sold their booty mostly for gold, food, and materials needed for forging and weapon crafting. These raids became possible because of their longboats, the primary mode of transport that became synonymous with Vikings as of today.

The first-ever recorded Viking raid in the British Isles occurred in year 793, wherein the monastery in Lindisfarne was raided and pillaged. Two years after that, the monastery in Rathlin Island was sacked as well. These raids happened not only because of the fact that Vikings are pagans (not Christian); monasteries are known to be the richest source of goods as well as slaves. [5]

How Viking Raids are Done

Believed to be done in a hit-and-run style, Viking raids are executed at a fast pace. Once they set their eyes on their target (mostly monasteries), the Vikings will land their longboats near their target. Longboats are preferred by Vikings because of their 'ramming' capabilities, so landing near sandbars or rocky areas doesn't pose many problems.

After the landing is done, the Vikings divide into smaller raiding teams, whose numbers vary depending on their target. Most of the time, the Viking leader attacks the target monastery along with the primary team while others pillage the nearby villages for potential slaves and goods. After that, they sack the entire location and carry their booty back to their longboats. These Viking raids mostly happen to a certain location at least once a year, unless it is really rich with booty.

Vikings are known far and wide for their brutality and harsh treatment towards their prisoners. That is the main reason why Viking raids are feared as well as hated by people during that time. However, not all Viking raids are successful. According to various historical records, some raids in Ireland were repelled such as in Ulaid in year 811 as well as in Munster and Connaught the next year.

It is probably because of this reason that the succeeding raids intensified, making it more ferocious and terrifying than it was before. At first, a raid only consists of three or four longboats and lasts for a week or two (or until their longboats run out of space for their booty) before returning to Scandinavia. This time, however, the Vikings brought fifty to a hundred (depending on their target location's size) longboats, landed on shores and set up their camps nearby. They attacked, pillaged and sacked Irish fortresses, monasteries, churches, and farms as well as the surrounding countrysides for months. According to records, these kinds of raids started in the year 836 and lasted for fifteen years. During this time, Irish kings were unable to repel such raids, resulting to most of the populace as well as monks getting enslaved and their goods looted in addition to their territories getting sacked.

After almost all of the intensified raids died down, the Irish initiated their counterattack and were successful in regaining some of their lost territories. In year 848 (three years before the last intensified Viking raid), the Irish regained Cork, which became a Viking town during that time. They also regained Vadrefjord (864), Youghal (866) and Dubhlinn (902), which was a great merchant town by then, driving the Vikings to the Isle of Man.

These Irish victories, however, were short-lived. In year 914, the Vikings initiated a second intensified raid in Vadrefjord, successfully retaking the location. Next, they attacked Leinster and Munster the following year through a series of offensive attacks while pillaging the monasteries in Lismore, Aghaboe, and Cork. In year 917, they successfully retook Dubhlinn. The second intensified raid stopped in the year 950, in which Vikings had stopped their raids in Ireland, settled in the towns they built for themselves and became traders.

Viking Appearances

The Vikings coming from Norway landed in Dublin. Without warning, they attacked and raided Ireland. So, instead of being ranked as sacred people, poets suddenly became equal with the laborers.

The first known Viking raid happened in 795 B.C. when the Vikings left Norway for Ireland -a more promising land. The earliest Viking raiders mostly came from the western Norway fjords. Their route was sailing down Scotland's Atlantic coast then over to Ireland. They also sailed to the Irish west coast, to the Skellig Islands off the coast of County Kerry during their early raids. These raids became the reason why the Christian Irish culture had their golden age interrupted and led to two hundred years of war. The Vikings also destroyed a number of towns and monasteries all over Ireland.

Viking Settlement

As winter months came, the Vikings settled along Irish coasts, and Ireland became their winter playground. They settled in Dublin, Cork, Arklow, Limerick, Wexford, and Waterford. In Kilmainham (in the west side of Dublin), archaeological evidence shows that there was a small Viking settlement in the mid- 840's A. D. in Ireland. There were also Irish journals that described the Vikings' inland movement often by the rivers' way (e. g. Shannon River) and back to their coastal settlements.

Among the Vikings, Thorgest was the first to put up an Irish kingdom. He sailed up the Shannon and the river Bann to Armagh in 839 A.D. where he carved out a kingdom containing Connacht, Meath, and Ulster. Thorgest's glory lasted for 6 years just when some of his subjects had enough. He was caught and drowned by the king of Mide, Màel Sechnaill mac Mail Ruanaid in Lough Owen.

After Thorgest's death, as high king, Màel Sechnail defeated a Norse army at Sciath Nechtain. He contacted the emperor of France, Charles the Bald asking to be allies as Christians against pagans. Unfortunately, it turned out to be unsuccessful and was a poor decision made. The Vikings erected a strong fortress in place of (the modern-day) the city of Dublin in 852 A. D. One of them declared himself as king, and they established a stronghold at Waterford the following year.

The Norse also built a fortified settlement near the Avoca River's mouth (modern-day Arklow in Wicklow County). According to the Annals of Ulster, Arklow was already occupied by 836 A.D. when the attack of the Vikings at Kildare was recorded.

Viking settlements in Ireland began earnestly in 914 A.D. When Waterford was taken; it became the first Irish city. It was the settlement of a Viking named Regnall. One can find the Tower of Reginald (Ireland's oldest civic building) here. Waterford was also the only Irish city that still has its Viking name retained.

Windy fjord or Ram fjord's name was originally Cuan na Gréine before it was called Harbour of the sun by the Irish. Wexton, Cork, Limerick, and Dublin were urbanized between 915-922 A.D. Modern excavations also proved of heavy Viking existence in Waterford and

31

Dublin. The Norse (means foreigner in Irish), a mixed Viking and Irish group began to influence Ireland after generations of plunder and courtship.

Even as of present, one can still trace Norse descents from among the residents of Irish coasts that have actual DNA evidence.

Viking Period's Everyday Life

The Viking raids made this a period of terror for Irish, especially to those who belonged to the Ecclesiastical communities. Being the primary target for booty, monasteries and churches became subject to periodic raids in which, some of these died and failed to resurrect even after this period. However, most of the monasteries and their structures remain intact, sparing themselves from the raider's wrath. This is probably due to the fact that Vikings knew that they will be filled with booty again, making it possible to initiate another raid sometime in the future.

Even the grad Fhene (commoners) weren't spared by the raids either. Even if their mud walls, as well as ditches, are enough to repel some Irish attacks, these defenses were practically useless against Vikings, who attack and raid in large numbers. Because of this, crannogs, as well as ringforts, became obsolete during the year 900s. Instead, these two were replaced by souterrains, which are heavily-defended underground chambers that are used mainly as places of refuge against Viking raiders. Because souterrains are practically hidden from enemy eyes, there are at least 3500 of those that managed to survive throughout Ireland.

If souterrains protected the common folk from raiders, monks and other members of the ecclesiastical community were protected by round towers during that time. Cylindrical in shape, round towers are defensive fortifications which had their entrances placed one floor high and are only accessible by ladder. In case of a Viking raid, the monks in the monastery will take as much food and valuables as they could, climb inside the tower, pull up its ladder before keeping it shut. Even if the raiders manage to enter the tower, the monks will just retreat upstairs, pulling the ladders up to restrict access. In the end, raiders either just gave up the pursuit or smoke the monks to their deaths.

End of Viking Rule

Due to the joint forces of the king of Meath and Brian Boru (941-1014 A. D.), the rule of Viking ended in Ireland. Brian Boru of mid-western Ireland gained influence through political conquests and maneuvers around the late 10th century. After he claimed the title of High King, he and his allies defeated the Vikings in 1014 at the Battle of Clontarf. When Boru was killed in battle, the Vikings lost their control over all Ireland and the Norse who remained became part of the Irish people. For 150 years, Ireland was free from invasion, but infighting weakened and drained the country from resources.

The Abbott of Clonmacnoise wrote a famous book in 1150. The book was entitled Chronicum Scotorum, and it was the story of Ireland from the Great Flood to the 12th century. The Normans (1167-1185) Ireland became a country with divided kingdoms by the 12th century. A few powerful regional dynasties fought against each other to gain control over all Ireland.

Ireland Lordship (1185-1254)

Seated at the southern banks of Shannon River, King John's castle was built in the 12th century.

Meanwhile, the Normans owned immense portions of Irish lands. They forefended the whole eastern coast from Waterford up to eastern Ulster, including Dublin as years passed. They also had gone as far west as Mayo and Galway. On the other hand, King John of England- Lord of Ireland warded the Norman regions and at the same time ensured that the Irish kings were under his power. Many Irish kings owed their armies and thrones to King John.

The Rise and Death of Brian Boru

Brian Boruma, or simply Brian Boru, came into power when his brother Mathgamain, Lord of the Dal Cais, was assassinated by the Christian Vikings of Limerick. At first, the Vikings were tolerated since they were more or less a peaceful lot even though their territory lies near the mouth of Shannon River. So after his brother's death, Brian Boru started his conquest of Ireland by killing the Vikings of Limerick, thereby avenging his brother.

Even though he's a Christian himself, he cared less about observing sacred traditions, leading his men right inside the monastery in Scattery Island, slaughtering King Imar and his sons who took refuge inside before desecrating the whole monastery. Because of what he did, Limerick became part of Munster. Four years after the death of his brother (in year 980), he also surpassed Eoganacht and declared himself as king of whole Munster. After that, he and his army eventually penetrated Laigin (Leinster) and Connacht through the help of Vikings of Vadrefjord.

Because of his exploits, the Ui Neill, which is the influential dynasty during that time, became alarmed of Brian Boru, eventually deciding to declare war with him. King Mael Sechnaill II, the leader of Ui Neill, fought Brian Boru by trying various tactics but eventually gave up after more than a decade of failed attempts. After their meeting at Clonfert, the two kings decided to divide Ireland, granting Brian Boru High Kingship over all of Munster as well as Dubhlinn (Dublin) and Laigin (Leinster). He, on the other hand, retained the allegiance of his own province and of Connaught for himself. However, the Viking King of Dublin and the lords of Laigin revolted

34

under his rule two years after. Brian Boru retaliated by defeating Laigin at Glenn Mama and descended into Dublin the following winter, burning down its fortress. Because of this, King Silkenbeard of Dublin submitted himself and became Brian Boru's supporter. King Mael Sechnaill II also submitted himself to Brian Boru in the year 1002 because of their influential decline as well as the rising influence of Shannon River when it comes to Viking trade.

By the year 1005 and 1006, Brian Boru's power was almost complete. However, he was killed during the Battle of Clontarf in 1014 even though he managed to suppress Dublin and Laigin's second revolt. But regardless of what had happened, not only did his victory did secure Irish hold in both Laigin and Dublin for more than two centuries; he also managed to end the weakening Viking's power and influence in all of Ireland, eventually returning the whole country to the Irish for good during his time.

The Period of Dynastic Upheaval

Ireland had experienced dynastic upheaval right after the death of Brian Boru in the year 1014. Right after the Battle of Clontarf and upon confirming Brian Boru's death, King Mael Sechnaill II of the Ui Neill dynasty reasserted himself as High King of all Ireland. However, after his death eight years later, all of the existing dynasties fought against one another, eventually resulting in confusion and almost endless power struggle.

During the 11th century, Ireland's politics became similar to the rest of Europe. Rulers spend their time away from home and fought battles instead, leaving the kingdom to their stewards who, in turn, employ other essential staff in the name of royalty that will operate inside the palace. On the other hand, governors were appointed by kings to oversee their territories' everyday operations such as the collection of taxes as well as observing laws and edicts.

Warfare also improved during this time. In addition to existing Viking technologies that they acquired in the past, the Irish also learned mounted and naval warfare, which eventually led to the use of Admiralty as well as Cavalry. These posts were granted by the kings to their subservient lords, lords who were expected to be loyal to them at all times.

From the year 1086 to 1114, the High Kingship was under dispute. It was during this time wherein the kings of Munster and Ui Neill became mortal enemies just like their ancestors. However, the situation changed when Connacht's successor, Turlough O'Connor came to power. Using his large army and navy, he succeeded in destroying the power of Munster between the years 1115 and 1131 before spending the rest of his reign in trying to become Ireland's High King. The task of accomplishing this, however, was passed to his son Rory after his death in the year 1156.

After succeeding his father's throne, Rory O'Connor knew that he had to conquer Dublin (Dublin) to become High King in all of Ireland. This conquest became difficult due to the fact that King Muirchertach Mac Lochlainn of the Ui Neill and King Dairmait Mac Murchada of Leinster were allies and both have their eyes on the High Kingship as well. However, when the king of Ui Neill was assassinated by his own vassals in the year 1166, the citizens of Dublin had allied themselves with King Rory. With their help, King Rory had managed to capture Ui Neill as well as Leinster and drove the remaining enemy, King Dairmait Mac Murchada, out of Ireland.

Christian Church Reformation

The Christian church in Ireland had reached its peak of glory even before Vikings had entered the country. This is proved by the monasteries having amassed huge, if not exorbitant, amount of wealth. It may have been a good thing for them at first. However, this is the main reason why Vikings are targeting them most of the time.

During and after the time of Vikings, the Christian church does not only suffered material losses; most of them became corrupt and entertained secular thoughts. In addition to the fact that the church became decentralized, making every abbot in monasteries too powerful, some members of the ecclesiastical community do practice indecent and unchristian behavior: accepting bribes, acquiring concubines for themselves and, most of all, many of these abbots were not even churchmen, let alone Christian. If there were those who still observe sound doctrine during this time, they were just a minority and don't have any influence in church organization.

When the early period of medieval age came, the Christian church reformation in Ireland was initiated by some members of the ecclesiastical community along with the church in Europe, who was busy reforming the French church during that time. The revival in monasticism had influenced the whole continent, effectively bringing Ireland under their control. The Cistercian Order was the first medieval order to establish their base of operations in Ireland, founding abbeys while observing sound Christian doctrine at the same time. Other monastic orders came after them, who also found new abbeys as well as seizing control of the old ones run by corrupt abbots.

To establish English control over the country, the Archbishop of Canterbury in England planned to assert his control over the church there, having established a relationship with the church in Dubhlinn(Dublin). However, the reformed Irish church was organized under the Archbishop of St. Patrick's monastery during that time, which was supported by the synods of Cashel in 1101, Rath Breasail in 1111 and Kells-Mellifont in 1152, much to the Archbishop of Canterbury's dismay.

Because of the Christian reformation, the Irish Church was divided into dioceses, their leaders and members being required to observe sound doctrine at all times and, most of all, the monasteries were stripped of their rights to own much land. Even though this reformation had successfully removed most of the corruption in churches as well as monasteries, it also destroyed the basis of most Irish poetry and learning during that time.

Chapter 5: The Normans in Ireland

Following the defeat of the Vikings in the early part of the 11th century, the Irish immediately engaged in a series of battles to gain control of the territory as well as assert their authority. For 150 years, there was continuous unrest until in 1150, the majority of Ireland was controlled by four powerful clans:

- The O'Neills in Ulster
- The O'Briens in Munster (family of Brian Boru)
- The O'Connors in Connaught
- The McMurrough (Led by Dermot McMurrough who also held Leinster)

As soon as Rory O'Connor takeover the leadership of Connacht, he begins to seize Munster from the O'Breins, but McMurrough was able to dominate a nominal portion of Dublin which is an important trading center of Ireland at that time having the support of the O'Neills. However, things changed when the ruler of Ulster was assassinated in 1166 resulting in a power struggle in the North which left Dermot McMurrough without any strong support. Rory O'Connor grabs the opportunity and seizes Dublin first before also taking over Leinster. After his defeat, McMurrough left Ireland and O'Connor was soon recognized as High King of Ireland.

The Normans in Ireland

For a short period, Ireland gains peace but while in England, McMurrough was preparing for his return to Ireland. With promises of land and influence, he sought for the support of King Henry II of England along with other powerful English allies. He was able to gain the strong support of the powerful Earl of Pembroke, Richard de Clare, also known as Strongbow.

It was in 1170 when Strongbow first landed in Ireland with an army of skilled and well-armed men in addition to some loyal supporters of McMurrough. This troop will work for the reinstatement of McMurrough as King of Leinster.

Strongbow married Aoife, the daughter of McMurrough which sealed the alliance along with a promise that he would succeed to the throne and so he did in May of the year 1171. However, King Henry did not welcome the quick and increasing rise to power of his once loyal subject. He considered Strongbow as a threat and an affront to his authority. In August of the same year, King Henry set foot on Irish soil in a fleet of 400 ships and well-equipped army. This is the first time in history that an English monarch ever visited Ireland.

Being guided by his practical considerations, Strongbow met the King on the way to Dublin, where he pledged his renewed allegiance, and thus he was able to retain his lands. At this point, the other remaining kings including Rory O'Connor saw the King as an ally in curtailing the power of Strongbow.

The Treaty of Windsor

It was in 1175 when the Treaty of Windsor was made, giving Henry the authority to overlord all territories already inhabited by the Normans. Strongbow as a subject of the king held onto Leinster. Rory O'Connor had sworn loyalty to the crown and was paying an annual levy. To implement the treaty, the King assigned military commanders and awarded them lands to own. Not soon enough, they sought to expand the territory they owned. Being left by themselves, they have taken control of a significant portion of Munster and Connacht in 1178 with John de Courcy as their leader. They soon attempted to conquer the land of the Ulster in the North.

By the middle of the 13th century, the power of the once great clans diminished as the Normans were able to control the majority of Ireland.

Although the O'Neill managed to protect Ulster by not allowing the Normans to take a foothold of their territory although they were able to control the East Coast, with the ongoing battles, the O'Neill can lose their dominant position. The part of the province not occupied by the non-Normans is divided between 12 other families.

The Native Irish

Before the arrival of the Normans in Ireland, all the lands were considered communal. While there are chieftains controlling territorial areas and expect people living under them to contribute food and engage in fighting, yet the lands never belong to anyone. However, with the arrival of the Norman, the concept of land property was definitely changed. Aside from introducing the concept of land ownership, they likewise make the native people of Ireland believed that the lands belong to them.

Soon enough, Irish farmers who had been cultivating their lands for a long period of time became tenants and have to pay rents and taxes to the Norman rulers so they can continue working on the land. This situation continued with horrifying consequences.

To defend their properties and established themselves, the Norman began building enormous castles. Inevitably, intermarriage occurred and that a new ruling class emerged with a mixture of Norman and Irish heritage.

In England at this time, the Normans gradually adopt the Irish language, dress, and laws. However, these were largely despised as 12 parliaments sat in Kilkenny against these and worked for the stopping or reverse this cultural integration.

Under the Statutes of Kilkenny which the parliament was working were various measures curbing further assimilation including forbidding Normans to subject under the Irish law, to use the Irish language, to intermarry with the Irish or to give Irish names to their children. However, this did not work out as planned for even while Ireland is nominally under the King's rule, a large portion of Ireland was still operating independently of the English crown.

During the last part of the 15th century, only the area surrounding Dublin remained under the direct control of the English. This area was then recognized as "The Pale" which is translated in Latin as "palus" meaning border or fence. In fact, there was an attempt to separate this part from the rest of the Ireland areas.

Within the Pale, the English rule still prevailed but for the rest of the Irish Normans, they behave independently, thus the idiomatic expression, "beyond the pale" is used to describe unacceptable or uncontrollable behavior. Over the years, the English likewise show their intolerance to the situation which leads to their struggle to maintain their identity.

The Anglo-French Invasion

In 1176, Strongbow dies, and King Henry took over Leinster but granted all his rights as Lord of Ireland to Prince John, the youngest among his sons. Prince John was the Lord of England until he was crowned as King of England in 1199. [6]

There was extensive colonization in the lands where the Anglo-Saxon had settled. Agricultural lands were established, and goods are sold in local markets, nationally, and extended even to Europe. People from other parts of Europe such as French, Welsh, and Belgian, in addition to the English, came to settle in the lands owned by Anglo-French Lords. The remaining Irish were then assigned as serfs working on the estates. Changes in the life of the poor Irishmen were noticeable, but for the rich Irish, their lifestyle remains the same.

The colonization of the Anglo-French in Ireland continued until the end of the 1200s. The Irish Kings remain submissive to the power of the foreign invaders, but the people were hoping for the coming of someone who will come and liberate them from the hands of their oppressors – the Anglo-French.

In 1176, Strongbow dies, and King Henry took over Leinster but granted all his rights as Lord of Ireland to Prince John, the youngest among his sons. Prince John was the Lord of England until he was crowned as King of England in 1199.

The Anglo-French ruled over Meath and Leinster by 1177. There was extensive colonization in the lands where the Anglo-Saxon had settled. Agricultural lands were established, and goods are sold locally, nationally, and even to Europe. People from other parts of Europe such as French, Welsh, and Belgian, in addition to the English, came to settle in the lands owned by Anglo-French Lords. The remaining Irish were then assigned as serfs working on the estates. Changes in the life of the poor Irishmen were noticeable, but for the rich Irish, their lifestyle remains the same.

The Anglo-French were expanding their colony, and it took off when John de Courcy invaded and ruled over Ulaid which was later known as Ulster. The O'Brien kingdom in eastern Munster was granted to William de Burgh, and Philip of Worcester, and Theobold Walter in 1185 who later founded the Butler Dynasty that played a significant role in the Irish history. It took them eight long years to subdue the region – later known as Osmond.

The colonization of the Anglo-French in Ireland continued until the end of the 1200s. The Irish Kings remain submissive to the power of the foreign invaders, but the people were hoping for the coming of someone who will come and liberate them from the hands of their oppressors – the Anglo-French.

The longest war from the year 1226-1235 happened in Western

Ireland. Richard de Burgh invaded the Irish Kingdom of Connacht but did not expect that the Irish were able to develop their military facilities since the time of Strongbow that it took them long and hard winning the battle.

It was also during this period when the FirzGerals or Geraldines conquer north Kerry and Waterford and later owned more lands in Kerry, Connacht, and Fermanagh. The FitzGerald built a castle at Belleek, Fermanagh which the locals burned and getting back control over Fermanagh.

By the mid-13th century, Hugh de Lucy died, and so the Irish kings – Donegal and Tyrone stopped paying tribute to the English to which the King made little response. This motivates the Irish kings to form an alliance with the King of Connacht. In 1259, They entered Ulster by force and killed the colonists and burning downtowns. The revolution was extending to Mu8inster where the Irish residing in there revolted against the Anglo-French Lords. In 1261, the Irish were able to defeat the English army sent by the king to avenge the colonists. The revolt quickly fizzled out when key leaders were killed in battles.

After the revolution, Walter de Burgh, also Lord of Connacht was granted the title as Earl of Ulster. In 1296, Walter de Burgh became the ruler of all Connacht and the whole of Ulster. He was next in power to the King of England. In the south, emerging families were the Butlers of Osmond and the Geraldines of Desmond. Leinster at this time was divided into smaller Lordships as the families divided their lands among their heirs.

Meath, on the other hand, was divided into two – the Trim and Meaths while the Lordship of Leinster was divided into four parts – the liberties of Kilkenny, Wexford, Carlow, and Kildare.

Restraint of Norman Invasion

The Normans had undergone sequential events that resulted in the downshift and eventually stopped their settlement and power in Ireland. The English Lordships were attacked by Gaelic rebels that relied on raids and surprise attacks. Because of this, many Norman knights were killed, Norman resources were put to strain, and many Gaelic chieftains had their territories returned. At the same time, Norman colonists lost their English financial resource as King Henry III and Edward I, his successor, was occupied with warring factions in Wales, Scotland, and England. There was chaos within Norman ranks, and Norman lords fought each other.

On the other hand, residents and settlers were pulled closer to the heart and spirit of the Irish countryside by the new strength of Gaelic Ireland and West European politics. Ireland faced a transition during the late 12th to the early 13th century: from acquisition of lordship to colonialism. Norman Invasion produced numerous castles, borough towns, import tenants, churches and an increase in commerce and agriculture. Changes became permanent as the Normans altered Gaelic society with productive land usage.

Irish lifestyle elevated (in some ways) and most Irish people in Leinster and Munster even have Norman surnames. Not only Irish people were influenced by the Normans. Normans also acquired the DNA, language, and Irish customs.

Norman Declination, Gaelic Revival and the Black Death (1254-1536)

There were three significant events in the 14th century of Irish history.

Edward Bruce of Scotland Irish Invasion

Bruce rallied Irish lords against the presence of Englishmen in the country in 1315. He suffered defeat at the battle of Faughart, near Dundalk. Though his troops caused massive destruction especially in populous areas of Dublin, the local Irish lords won back their lands (in the midst of chaos) that were generations lost to their families.

Murder of William Donn de Burgh, 3rd Earl of Ulster (June 1333)

His land was divided among his family, and those in Connacht openly sided with the Irish and rebelled against the English crown. So, all of Ireland that is west of Shannon River turned to the Normans and was completely lost to the English rule. Then, the Burkes allied with the Dublin administration after more than 200 years.

Black Death During Medieval Times (1348)

Black Death landed on Irish shores and struck the English and Normans that resided in towns and villages the most. The Irish that lived in rural places were luckily unaffected. According to a celebrated account in chronicles of Kilkenny (Cill Chainnaigh), from a monastery, it described the plague as the beginning of human extinction and the end of the world.

Gaelic Irish language dominated after the plague ended. The English dominated area became constricted to the Pale- a fortified region around Dublin. Norman lords that lived outside the Pale adopted Irish customs and language so as to save their own skins. They became more Irish than the Irish (according to some people) and were known as the Old English. They sided with the native Irish against England in military and political conflicts during the next centuries, and they became Catholics after the Reformation.

Inside the Pale, authorities became alarmed that the whole of Ireland would become Irish. So, in 1367, they passed The Statutes of Kilkenny- special legislation that banned those of English descent to speak the Irish language, wear Irish clothing and inter-marriage with Irish people. This gained least attention and followers as their government in Dublin had almost zero authority.

The control of the government in Dublin continued to decrease during the 15th century. This time, England was engaged with their own affairs in the War of The Roses. Many English kings commissioned the powerful Fitzgerald, Earls of Kildare, authority over their territories. As time passed, the English monarchy became remote to Irish politics. As the Gaelic lords expanded their powers, they decreased English rule in Dublin.

Chapter 6: Ireland During 15th -16th Century

The Church Reformation

Throughout the medieval period and even until the 20th century, the church plays a significant role in Irish society as well as in their culture. At this point, the churches were fairly distributed across Ireland ruled by native Irish lords and also those lands ruled by Anglo-French lords that it was, therefore, difficult to rule over the land and assert control over churches. The King of England had, in fact, attempted to place Anglo-French Bishops over all dioceses in their lands. However, this was met with great condemnation by the Pope who expressed his outrage over such discrimination.

Dating back from the Normans invasion of Ireland, the title, "Lord of Ireland" was used by the Normans and English monarchs to refer to their Irish conquests. The Crown of Ireland Act in 1542 has renamed Ireland as the Kingdom of Ireland and granted King Henry the title as the King of Ireland. This was done through the command of King Henry himself as the Lordship of Ireland was granted by the Papacy. Worried that his title as the Lord of Ireland would be withdrawn by the Pope as he had been excommunicated twice - in 1533 and 1538, he mapped this out. [7][8]

The King further arranged that he would be declared to head the Church in Ireland with George Brown, the Archbishop of Dublin as the main instrument in the establishment of the state church in the Kingdom of Ireland who was appointed by the King upon the death of the incumbent bishop even without the Pope's approval. He arrived in Ireland in 1536.

With King Henry's death in 1547, reforms were continued by his successor – Edward VI of England. When the Church of Ireland likewise considers Apostolic succession for continuity in the hierarchy, the Roman Catholic Church disputed this claim asserting that only bishops approved by and in communion with the Holy See are considered legitimate. [9]

Edward the IV of England

Edward the VI of England, son of King Henry formally established Protestantism as the state religion. As his father reformation had been political, the son was as much religious but he reign only for six years and his principal reform act had much less impact in Ireland. [10][11]

Queen Mary of England

When Queen Mary I of England ascent to the throne in 1953 - being a faithful Roman Catholic - reversed Henry and Edward's efforts in the past. She imposed orthodox Roman Catholicism and then married Philip of Asturias who became the King of Spain in 1958. [12]

The Queen arranged for the Act of Supremacy which asserted England as being independent of Papal authority to be repealed resulting to forcing the dismissal of bishops in possession of diocese formerly appointed by her father without the Pope's approval. However, monasteries remain dissolved in the preservation of the loyalty of those who purchased monastic lands.

Soon enough, Queen Mary started planning for the mass confiscation of Irish lands for settlers from Great Britain. In 1955, Mary and Philip were granted the papal bull to reconfirm their position as the Catholic King and Queen of Ireland.

Queen Elizabeth

In 1959, when Queen Elizabeth, half-sister of Queen Mary I succeeded the throne, she managed to pass another act of Supremacy in 1959 declaring the English crown as the supreme head of the Church in England in place of the pope and that any act of allegiance to the pope will be considered a treason because the papacy is claiming both political and spiritual powers over those who are following him.

The English Regained Control over Ireland

Two of the most influential families in Ireland were the Fitzgeralds who resided in south-west Ireland and the Butlers who lived in Tipperary. Despite being descended from Norman settlers, both of these families had long lived in Ireland, and they already considered themselves Irish by heart. Unfortunately, these two families have a totally different perspective when it comes to the Englishmen. More than any other families in Ireland, the Fitzgeralds cultivated pure hostility to the English. The Butlers, on the other hand, supported the English king. In 1463, one of the FitzGerald earls showed support to the English. For this, he was captured by his own relatives and was murdered in 1468.

Because of this failed attempt to expand England's jurisdiction in other parts of Ireland, the English began to collaborate with Kildare's Earl Garrett Mór (also known as Gerald FitzGerald) who governed the western border of the Pale. This alliance between the English King and the earl brought great advantages to both parties—with Garrett Mór gaining more power and influence in Ireland as its Lord Deputy, and the king gaining control over the earl's territory.

In 1485, King Henry VII ascended the throne in England through the support of the Butlers despite the opposition from many of the Irish lords including Earl Garrett Mór of Kildare who supported the previous king. King Henry VII didn't like how Garrett Mór gained so much influence and power in Ireland that he was becoming a huge threat to the English authority in Pale. The newly crowned king then decided that it was high time to re-establish their control over Ireland like how the Normans had once relished it 250 years prior to his reign.

The relationship between the King and the earl of Kildare even got worse in 1487 when the latter supported Henry's rival to the throne, Edward, and even acknowledged him as the rightful heir to the English throne. Henry went livid with rage and had Garrett Mór abducted and imprisoned in the Tower of London for treason. After that, he immediately passed a law putting an end to the independence of the Irish Parliament in the Pale. Instead, London itself will have direct authority over Ireland.

Unfortunately, the monarch soon realized that he couldn't control the other lords in Ireland without the help of Earl Garrett Mór of Kildare. He then begrudgingly reinstated Garrett Mór as the Lord Deputy in 1496 knowing that if he could control the earl, he would have a better chance of spreading the English authority all over Ireland.

In 1513, Garrett Mór was succeeded by his son, Garrett Og. The son continued his father's rule as the Lord Deputy of Ireland in the reign of King Henry VIII, the son of Henry VII. Unfortunately for Garrett Og, his influence over Ireland began to decline with the king's marriage to the daughter of the FitzGerald's rival family, the Butlers.

Garrett Og was summoned to London in 1533, and because of this, a false rumor circulated that the Lord Deputy was executed. At the same time, Garrett Og's son also declared that he would no longer inherit the title as the succeeding Lord Deputy of Ireland. To top that, the Kildares were murdered and their castle destroyed. The territory owned by the Earl of Kildare was added to the Pale (currently known as the Kildare County). From then on, only

Englishmen ruled the Pale and ending all the chances of Irish Lords to claim the title.

Since there are almost no loyal supporters left from the Irish Lords, King Henry VIII was forced to compromise and resort to a more peaceful policy. He signed peace treaties with many Irish Lords, and in return, they swore their loyalty to the English throne. This diplomatic tactic managed Henry to gain control of most parts of Ireland immediately.

Ireland in the Tudor Dynasty

During the sixteenth century, Ireland was controlled by different governments. Some parts were ruled by various Gaelic chiefs together with their families known as clans. These people follow their own customs, laws, and language. On the other hand, many groups from Leinster, Munster, and Pale swore their loyalty to the English monarch; thus, they follow the English customs and law.

In 1541, King Henry VIII of England from the family of Tudors went against the Pope and gave himself the title King of Ireland with the support from prestigious families like the O'Neill. This led to an increase of English immigration and settlement in the country. Furthermore, the Irish and Gaelic chiefs who supported the English king gained titles in exchange for their loyalty and observance of the English laws. King Henry gave his word that their direct family line would stay in power. By the time of his death in 1547, the forty Gaelic lords who pledged their loyalty had been given English titles. Two of these famous clans, the O'Donnell and O'Neill, were given the title of earls.

The arrangement worked quite well for some time, but the Gaelic lords revolted against the king because of the overwhelming demands of the Tudor monarchs. As the king's retaliation and also in compliance with the English law, their lands were confiscated.

The Tudors met strong resistance from the Gaelic lords. Some of them even attacked English loyalists and supporters particularly those who live in the Pale including parts of Louth, Meath, and Kildare.

The English Immigrants to Ireland and the Tudor Plantations

During their respective reigns, Queen Mary I (1553-1558) and Queen Elizabeth I (1558-1603) decided that the English must gain more power in Ireland. For this feat, they resorted to sending more loyal subjects to Ireland by granting them confiscated lands which were later identified as plantations. The loyal immigrants, on the other hand, were called settlers or planters.

From 1556 to 1557, Queen Mary 1 (also known as Mary Tudor) confiscated the lands of the Gaelic clans O'Connors and O'Mores and granted these lands to the English settlers. The new settlers got about two-thirds of the land while the native Irish were driven to the areas near Shannon which are known to be of poor quality. This, in turn, wreaked havoc between the new settlers and the Irish clans who fought back to regain their lands which continued for about 50 years.

The English settlers were forced to build stone houses and have their own weapon because of the attacks. They were also ordered not to marry into Irish families and even make them their servants. Additionally, they were forbidden to let Irish families rent in their land. Queen Mary 1 established that only loyal English subjects could live in plantation areas.

Queen Mary also ordered that the confiscated lands of O'Connors and O'Mores be divided into two counties; and that the Irish who lived west of the planted lands had to comply with the English laws. The Laois was renamed as Queen's County and its main town, Maryborough (currently Portlaoise). Even Offaly became King's County in honor of King Philip II who is the queen's husband. Its main town was also called Philipstown (currently Daingean).

When Queen Elizabeth I became the queen of England in 1558, she decided that Ireland is a strategic place to colonize. Aside from being in the same climate as her native England, Ireland is also targeted by the queen's archenemy, the Spanish Catholic monarch, King Philip. She feared that the latter would send forces to Ireland and use them to attack England.

Queen Elizabeth I decided to make Ireland more English by sending more immigrants, giving them lands at a cheap price. This way, the monarch can easily control the neighboring Gaelic lords and their clans. However, this step was met with resistance from the Irish natives. The revolt by the O'Neills of Tyrone (ended in 1561) and two attacks by the Fitzgeralds of Cork and Kerry (ended in 1575 and 1580 respectively). With the defeat of the Fitzgeralds in Cork, Elizabeth took this as an advantage and began to establish a plantation in Munster. The plantation that was once Fitzgerald's was quickly developed into towns and farming lands by 1587. Sadly, the settlement was devastated by a coordinated Irish attack in 1598, and it never recovered. Even so, many English settlers stayed behind in isolated areas.

The 1580 Rebellion

Prelude: The First Desmond Rebellion

Munster was ruled by the influential family of Desmond (branch family of Fitzgeralds in Munster), with its head being on friendly terms with Queen Elizabeth. However, the earl, together with some reputable families like the Fitzmaurices, found unrest with the English intrusion into the Desmond territories. They were also against the creation of the office of the governor (or Lord President) in the province of Munster as well as the favorable policies for the Butlers of Ormonde who are the Fitzgeralds' adversary; but what the

Desmonds could not accept was the government's unjust arrest of Earl Gerald, the head of the family, and his brother John in 1568 for being a part in a private war against the Butlers in 1565.

The First Desmond Rebellion began in 1569 led by the captain-general of the Fitzgerald army, James FitzMaurice FitzGerald, in the absence of Earl Desmond. However, he was defeated by the English forces with the support of the Butlers (led by the Third Earl of Ormonde, Thomas Butler).

Despite the rebellion, the English monarch pardoned the Desmonds and Fitzmaurice but has confiscated majority of the lands and properties of the family. In the aftermath of the First Desmond Rebellion, Fitzmaurice found himself impoverished and Earl Desmond was forbidden to demand military service. On top of these resentments, Fitzmaurice was a devout Catholic who had deep antagonism towards Protestantism, which had been introduced by the English. In 1575, James Fitzmaurice went to France to seek help from Catholic powers to restart another rebellion. He found support from the ruler of Spain, Philip II, and Pope Gregory XIII.

The Beginning

The start of 1580 rebellion (also known as the Second Desmond Rebellion) was marked with the assassination of two English officials namely, Arthur Carter and Henry Davells in a tavern in Tralee. John of Desmond and Fitzmaurice commanded about 3,000 men which include native Irishmen and a small number of European soldiers. However, their plans for encouraging more reinforcements were impeded by the efforts of Sir William Winter who seized the ships of foreign forces and interrupted their sea-routes.

Unfortunately, Fitzmaurice was killed at an encounter with Burkes of Clan William after his men stole some of the horses of Theobald Burke who was a cousin of Fitzmaurice. This incident left John of

Desmond as head commander of the rebellion. The rebels were able to take hold of the southern Munster as the English forces did not have enough troops to retake it. [13]

The Involvement of Earl Desmond

Nicholas Malby, the Lord President of Connaught, marched through the territory of the Desmonds and brought devastation in the countryside. He even demanded that Earl Desmond surrender his Askeaton castle, but the Irish lord refused his demand. With that, the earl was proclaimed as a traitor by the Lord Justice of Ireland, William Pelham. This meant that Earl Desmond should be captured and executed accordingly. Being a hunted man, the earl, along with the remaining Fitzgeralds, was forced to join the rebellion.

Earl Desmond claimed the leadership of the rebellion in quite a spectacular manner. He and his followers raided the town of Youghal, annihilating the English garrison there and hanging the officials for everyone to behold. They even went further by looting and abusing the civilians. The earl's force besieged the city of Cork before driving back into the mountains of Kerry. Meanwhile, the lord of MacCarthys, MacCarthy Mor, announced his joining by plundering Kinsale.

The English, in retaliation, sent Sir William Pelham, Sir George Carew, and Thomas Butler (the Third Earl of Ormonde) to subdue the rebels and devastate the Desmond territory in Cork, Limerick, and Kerry counties. They even killed civilians who lived in those areas in order to faze the followers of the Desmonds.

In the spring of 1580, the English forces took hold of the principal Desmond stronghold at Carrigafoyle Castle located by the Shannon river mouth. This move cut off the FitzGerald forces from the north of the country and blocked the landing of the foreign aid into the main Munster port of Limerick. When the news of the fall of

Carrigafoyle castle spread, the other Desmond forts were also easily destroyed. Many of the Irish lords including Mac Carthy Mor, Barry and Roche surrendered knowing that the English had the upper hand. By the summer of 1580, it might have looked like the rebellion had been completely obliterated; but it was again revived by the onset of the new rebellion in Leinster.

The Leinster Rebellion

In July 1580, Fiach McHugh O'Byrne from the Wicklow Mountains started the rebellion in the eastern part of Ireland. He collaborated with the local lords and clan leaders including the O'Tooles, O'Moores, and Kavanaghs. Many of them were already veterans in fighting the English garrisons. Furthermore, the rebels gave the epithet "King of Leinster" to Creon MacMurrough Kavanagh whose ancestors held this title even before the English invasion, as a sign of their rejection to the English crown. O'Byrne was later joined by Viscount Baltinglass, James Eustace, a marcher lord of the Pale who was motivated by his devotion in Catholicism.

In August, John Desmond and Nicholas Sanders met the Viscount Baltinglass in Laois in order to coordinate their troops. Unfortunately, both parties were unable to establish a common strategy, and there was limited assistance from the Barrow valley region. Nonetheless, the dawn of rebellion near the center of the English jurisdiction in Dublin was taken as an important concern to the English forces.

The former Lord Deputy of Ireland, Sir Henry Sidney, swayed the response from his membership of the Privy Council and a new Lord Deputy was dispatched from England together with 6,000 troops. The immediate order for the new deputy, Arthur Grey, 14th Baron Grey de Wilton, was to suppress the rebellion in Leinster.

On the 25th of August the same year, the English troops under the command of Baron Grey de Wilton were defeated by the combined forces of Viscount Baltinglass and Fiach McHugh O'Byrne. While they were trying to attack O'Byrne's fortress at Glenmalure in the midst of Wicklow Mountains, they were ambushed losing more than 800 soldiers in the process. William Stanley was then sent by the Baron Grey de Wilton to protect the Pale area of Leinster. O'Byrne and his allies were able to attack English settlements in the east and southeast but failed to advance their victory at Glenmalure.

During the rebellion and its aftermath, a number of people from Wexford and Pale were hanged as traitors. Amongst the persecuted were Margaret Ball (wife of the Lord Mayor of Dublin) and Dermot O'Hurley (the Catholic Archbishop of Cashel). These executions left a bitter taste in the Irish natives and resulted in the prolonged isolation of the Old English from the English state in Ireland.

Spanish and Papal Backing

On September 10, 1580, a squadron of Spanish ships headed by Don Juan Martinez de Recalde arrived with a Papal force of Spanish and Italian soldiers. The 600 Italian soldiers were under the command of Sebastiano di San Giuseppe (also known as Sebastiano da Modena) at Smerwick located on the Dingle Peninsula. The troops were sent by King Philip II to secretly assist the rebellion since it was financed by Pope Gregory. Earl Desmond, his brother John, and Baltinglass tried to collaborate with the expeditionary force but were intercepted by the forces under Grey and Ormonde. On the other side, Richard Bingham blocked off the ships sent by the Pope into the bay at Smerwick. As a result, San Giuseppe was left with no choice but to strengthen his men in the fort at Dún an Óir.

In October 1580, Baron Grey de Wilton with 4,000 of his troops landed at Smerwick and seized the garrison. The Papal forces were trapped at the tip of the narrow Dingle Peninsula, blocked by Mount Brandon on one side and the English force on the other. This means that the Spanish and Italian troops had no means of escape. Moreover, the English were geared up with heavy artillery by the sea which quickly destroyed the improvised fortress of Dún an Óir. After a three-day siege, the Italian commander surrendered on October 10, 1580. Baron Grey de Wilton ordered the execution of the Papal forces, sparing only the commanders. All the Spanish and Italian troops together with the Irish men and women were all beheaded and their bodies discarded into the bottom of the sea. English writer and explorer, Sir Walter Raleigh, was one of the English soldiers present during the siege and execution at Smerwick.

The Dusk of the Rebellion

The war extended for two more years with the civilian population as the sacrifice for all the bitter fighting. Their homes, crops, and livestock were all destroyed. Baron Grey de Wilton was described to be a heartless English commander. His black hat tactics include burning the civilian's corn, driving their cattle, and destroying their harvest. This resulted in famine, malnutrition, and plague.

Due to Grey's excessive brutality, Queen Elizabeth I removed him from the office as the Lord Deputy of Ireland. By mid-1582, it was reported that around 30,000 people died of famine in Munster and hundreds were dying in Cork city due to disease and starvation.

The rebellion slowly broke up. In April 1581, Elizabeth offered amnesty to the rebels except for their leaders. Many of the Desmonds' old-time supporters took this chance and surrendered. Meanwhile, Baltinglass escaped to France in August 1581. Fiach MacHugh O'Byrne made a false surrender in April 1581 but resorted into raiding after a short time. He surrendered for good in September 1582, finally ending the battle in Leinster. John Desmond was killed in a skirmish north of Cork in early 1582.

The Earl of Desmond himself was tracked down and killed in

Glenaginty in the Slieve Mish Mountains on November 11, 1583, by the Moriarty clan of Castledrum. The earl and his troops raided the property of the Moriarty, stole their livestock and even abused the sister of the clan chief. They were then chased after and killed in Glenaginty near Tralee in County Kerry. The rebellion was finally concluded in 1583 when the Earl of Ormonde took over the command of English forces. The earl used diplomatic approach to the campaign. He restrained the rebels to Kerry and West Cork, persuading many of the Desmonds to surrender.

Famine Memorial - Dublin

The Aftermath

Munster suffered from bubonic plague and famine for years after the Desmond rebellion. The population was greatly diminished, and the lands were left empty. About a third of the province's population died in the war.

Most areas in the Muster—about 300,000 acres of land— were confiscated by Queen Elizabeth. In 1585, the plantation in Muster was established, and new English settlers arrived to cultivate the land. Even huge estates were granted to some like Walter Raleigh. Many of these new settlers had a hard time finding the location of Muster and were also harassed by the local Irish, so they decided to return back home to England.

Ulster History Park

The Plantation of Ulster

At the dawn of 15th Century, Ireland became a place of mixed culture as well as races except for Ulster, which remained pure Celtic. Even though the rest of the country was a mixture of English, Viking, Celtic and Norman cultures, Ulster remained purely Celtic. It is due to the fact that this was the farthest place, making it safe against the Norman Invasion, as well as the reason that it was being defended by strong clans such as the O'Neills living in Tir Eoghain. And most of all, invaders were thinking that Ulster was not worth conquering.

It was during the year 1598 when Hugh O'Neill, the Earl of Tir Eoghain and his army decided to do a pre-emptive strike against the English, catching them off-guard. Because of this, he successfully drove the English out of Ulster. The English, however, decided to build forts around the southern part of the province, forcing the Irish to attack the forts instead. On December 24, 1601, O'Neill's army was defeated at the Battle of Kinsale, forcing him to retreat to his stronghold in Tir Eoghain (Tyrone nowadays). He did not surrender, however, so the English decided to strengthen their fortifications and destroyed Ulster's crops hoping to make him either attack again or surrender for good. In the year 1602, O'Neill and his army attacked again but were defeated at Omye (Omagh) by Lord Mountjoy and his men. A year later, O'Neill and the English signed a treaty in Mellifont, agreeing to the terms that his lands will remain under his possession, but he will revoke his Irish title as well as adopt English Laws in Ulster.

Despite the conditions in the Treaty of Mellifont, the English thought that it is not enough to make Ulster submissive towards their rule. They also knew that the Catholic Spain, who is allied with O'Neill, can supply Ulster with enough weapons in case they decided to revolt again. Because of this, the English resorted to a somewhat familiar solution: Plant Ulster with Protestant settlers. This time, however, the shortcomings of the previous plantations were all determined and applied with the right solution. The Laois/Offaly as well as Munster Plantations were greatly affected by Irish attacks, so they decided to build fortifications called Plantation Towns. By 1609, the English mapped the entire four million acres of land and gave it out a year later. It was then that the counties such as Antrim, Monaghan, and Down were planted privately. At the same time, English settlers were planted in Derry and Armagh while Tir Eoghain and Donegal were planted with Scots. Cavan and Fermanagh, on the other hand, were planted with both English and Scots.

Since most of the planted settlers were Scottish, these people brought Calvinism or Presbyterian teachings along with them. This is classified as Protestant, and their teachings are different from those of Catholic and Church of England (Anglican). Aside from Calvinism, the Scots also introduced a Puritan way of life as well as new farming methods, making Northeast Ireland very different from the rest. This made the native Ulstermen angry, resulting in the settlers getting attacked and their crops destroyed. But despite all of that, many Irishmen stayed and worked under the settlers, making the Ulster Plantation the most successful one as of date. [14]

Chapter 7: Cromwell and the Restoration

Oliver Cromwell led what is referred to in Irish history as the Cromwellian war in Ireland in 1649-1653 during the Wars of Three Kingdoms. Others called it the Cromwellian Conquest. Cromwellian.

Majority of the areas in Ireland were under the control of the Irish Catholic Confederation after the Irish Rebellion in 1641. In 1649, the English Royalists who were defeated by the Parliamentarians in the English Civil War created an ally with the Confederates until 1652 when Cromwell invaded Ireland on behalf of England Parliamentarians. This brought an end to the eleven-year war Irish Confederate Wars. However, the guerrilla warfare did not end with it and continued for about a year after this. The vast of the population at that time were Roman Catholics. Cromwell passed a series of Penal Laws that lead to the confiscation of the people's lands.

The reconquest of Ireland was too brutal that Cromwell was well-hated by the people. The impact of war on the people was too severe although there were no documented reports on the number of lives that were actually lost. After the war came a famine and the outbreak of bubonic plague. All these resulted in an extreme decline in the Irish population. The decline in population as a result of the Parliamentarian campaign was estimated to be within 15-83 percent range. Around 50,000 people were also transported out of the country as indentured laborers.

Cromwell was then too harsh on the Irish Catholics as a form of revenge for the rebellion of 1641 where Protestant settlers in Ulster were massacred. He likewise needed to raise a large amount of money to repay the London merchants who provided subsidies for the war under the Adventurers Act. Those implicated in the 1641 rebellion were executed while those who joined Confederate Ireland had their properties confiscated. Many were sent to West Indies as laborers. Confiscated lands owned by Catholic landowners who did not participate in the wars were allowed to claim their lands in Connacht.[15][16][17][18][19]

Catholics were not allowed to live in the towns, and the religious practice of Catholicism was completely banned and priests were executed. Irish soldiers who fought for the Confederates and Royalist armies which were estimated to be around 54,000 based on William Petty's estimate find services in the armies of Spain and France.

Prior to these wars, Catholics in Ireland owned about 60% of the lands but during the English restoration, only 20% of these lands remained in their ownership, and this percentage further declined to 8% during the Commonwealth period. After the 1660 restoration, Catholics were not allowed to serve in any public office with the exception of the Irish Parliament.

The Parliamentarian Campaign in Ireland was considered to be the most ruthless of the Civil War period particularly the presence of Cromwell at Wexford and Drogheda. However, there are arguments that his actions, if based on the standards at that time can't be considered as excessive cruelty. Those who are defending Cromwell even argued that his actions applied only to men in arms and that accounts of civilian massacres are still being disputed.

Regardless of the point of views, the campaign remains notorious in Irish history being responsible for the greatest death toll among Irish people. The cited reason was the counter-guerrilla tactics employed by Edmund Ludlow, Henry Ireton, and John Hewson against the Catholic population where they burn crops in large quantity and kill civilians forcing them to join movements.

Long-term Results

The Cromwellian conquest completed the British colonization of Ireland, which was merged into the Commonwealth of England, Scotland and Ireland in 1653–59. It causes the destruction of the native Irish Catholic who owned lands and replaced them with colonists with a British identity. The sufferings and hatred caused by the Cromwellian settlement was a powerful source of Irish nationalism from the 17th century onwards.

After the Restoration of the English monarchy during the Stuart period, Charles of England restored about one-third of confiscated lands to their former landlords through the Act of Settlement 1662 but lacked support from English parliamentarians, thus not all were restored.

Chapter 8: Ireland in the 18th -19th Century

In the 18th Century

Through Penal Laws, the colonists were able to accomplish their expected results. Within a few generations, the Irish were reduced to poverty as many were illiterate and unskilled. By the year 1750, 93% of the land that belongs to the Irish was transferred to non-Irish landowners. By the year 1770, they already owned almost 100 percent of the Irish lands. The Irish then was reduced to being a country of tenants.

Some eyewitness accounts of the life of an average Irish tenant farmer proved that the Irish peasant farmer is poor than the lowest serfs in German and Poland. Their life is one of deprivation and desperation. About half of those who lived in rural areas lived in small mud cabins with no windows. It was normal to see farm animals living in a cabin with the people. Only the abundance of peat helps these people to survive in the winter.

Lands that were once owned by the Irish were now being rented by them. In order to increase rental income derived from the land, greedy landlords are dividing and subdividing their lands, so families have less and fewer areas to live and paying more for the rental each time. The price of the rent is actually double the price one would pay if renting in England.

The farmers lived by growing potatoes, and many of them never tasted meat or bread. Their meals were always potatoes and sometimes include buttermilk.

All these inhuman treatments were not placidly accepted by the Irish and with the execution of the Penal Laws; their response was a sort of guerilla warfare carried out secretly.

In the 1760s, there were gangs of men wearing white shirts over their clothes; hence they were called "White boys" who roam the countryside at night burning barns, tearing down fences, and crippling cattle. They were also after tithes collectors, informers, and men of landlords torturing them to death. Landlord's houses and properties were being destroyed. There are also some reports of shooting through windows of manor houses. With these, landlords' houses were often barricaded and secured by stationed military men or soldiers.

By the end of the 19th century, the Irish started planning for the insurrection of 1798. The plan is for simultaneous revolts all over entire Ireland at the same time that a large army of French soldiers is about to land in Ireland. However, the ship carrying these soldiers ran into a strong storm as they are in sight of the land that most of these ships sank and were not able to reach the

The 1778 Rebellion

seashore. However, the Irish, armed with pikes and clubs push through with the revolt and did remarkably well against muskets and canons of their enemies. The battle occurred in Vinegar Hill in County Wexford. The Irish stood their ground, but then, the enemy had blown them up with cannon balls. Although the Irish lost the battle, it became an inspiration to the most popular Irish war song entitled, "The Boys of Wexford." In other parts of the country, many of the Irish were butchered while on their knees begging for mercy during the mopping-up operation of the colonists. In that war, more than 50,000 were killed, and the majority died in cold blood than in the battle.

Chapter 9: Modern Ireland

Ireland hasn't had Parliament on its own since 1801, only a handful of Irish Members of Parliament (MP) who sat in the Westminster parliament in London. Westminster decided not to give any compromises to the Catholics despite their exhibited persistence. In 1823, there was a radical move from the *Catholic Association* headed by Daniel O'Connell, a Catholic barrister, in order to urge the full liberty of the Catholics. It quickly turned into a political mass movement, forcing the London parliament to grant Catholic Emancipation by 1829 and practically freeing the Catholics from all their disadvantages.

O'Connell's success made him the most influential figure in Ireland, giving him more confidence to seek the revocation of the Act of Union of 1800 and the re-establishment of the Irish parliament. He designed the *Repeal Association* and based his campaign on that for emancipation. The agitation was identified as mass meetings with the attendance of hundreds to thousands of people. In 1843, the London Government gave its resistance by banning a Dublin rally of which O'Connell conceded his defeat. This memorialized the successful end of the repeal campaign.

In the 1840s, the group of Thomas Davis created the *Young Ireland* movement. Like the *United Irishmen*, the group aims to educate everyone who lived in Ireland to embrace their nationality regardless of their culture, faith, and roots. When the group staged an insurrection in 1848, everything came crumbling down. However, their expressed ideas strongly inspired and motivated the next generations about their concept of liberty.

The end of the European war in 1815 brought a drastic impact on the Irish economy. Due to the army needs for food supplies, tillage farming experienced relative growth during the warring times. Potatoes, in particular, became a staple. Unfortunately, the end of the war also marked the transition of tillage farming to pasture-based farming, causing agrarian unemployment in the process. There was also a population explosion of 8 million by 1841; two-thirds of this depended on agriculture alone. While Ireland was facing the uncertainty in the agrarian economy, the country yet had to face another blow to the economy—blight in potato cropping in 1845. This was followed by another failure in the following year to 1848 and coupled with severe weather, Ireland faced famine. By 1851, the population was reduced by about two million due to mixed factors like disease, starvation, and emigration of people to Britain and North America. [20]

Ireland in the second half of the nineteenth century was characterized by various campaigns for land reform and national independence. In 1858, the secret society of *Irish Republican Brotherhood (IRB)*, also known as the *Fenians*, was founded. Two of their most controversial leaders were John O'Leary and James Stephens. In 1867, the group organized an armed revolt. The members don't believe that diplomatic and constitutional attempts would bring them the goal they wanted to achieve. Nevertheless, the uprising was easily and quickly suppressed although the secret society still existed thereafter.

By the end of the nineteenth century, Ireland pursued the concept of cultural nationalism. In 1884, the *Gaelic Athletic Association* was founded, aiming to promote the national games. The *Gaelic League* (1893) founded by Eoin MacNeill and Douglass Hyde, attempted to restore the Irish language and culture nationwide. Simultaneously, Arthur Griffith established a new political party called *Sin Féin* ("We Ourselves") from 1905 to 1908. Its strategy centers on the conviction that Irish Members of Parliament should withdraw from the Westminster and build an independent parliament. The party had close ties with the IRB. In 1913, a socialist and separatist group called the *Irish Citizen Army* was created based on the Dublin labor dispute.

The Sin Féin representatives, headed by Éamon de Valera, then declared themselves as the first dependent Parliament (or *Dáil*) in Dublin. When the English tried to obliterate Sin Féin, it led to the War of Independence from 1919 to 1921. The Irish forces were commanded by Michael Collins. After more than two years of battle, a truce was agreed upon. The Anglo-Irish Treaty which was signed December 1921 stated that the 26 counties gained independence as the *Irish Free State*.

However, after the Free State had been established, a civil war between the newly found government and those who opposed the Treaty happened. Éamon de Valera led the opposition. Although the civil war ended in May 1923, it had claimed the lives of those who had led the campaign for independence including Cathal Brugha and Michael Collins.

Chapter 10: Ireland Today

Ireland or Irish Eire is a country located in Western Europe which occupies about five-sixths of the British Isles westernmost island.

While geographically isolated, the magnificent scenery of Ireland's coastlines faces the wide expanse of the Atlantic Ocean and has helped a lot in developing its rich heritage of culture and tradition initially linked to the Gaelic language.

The vast green-hued landscape of Ireland is responsible for the popular so-called "Emerald Isle."

Ireland is also famous for its treasured collections of folklore ranging from tiny leprechauns with hidden pots of gold to that of Saint Patrick who according to legend rid the island of snakes. Although many may have considered the country as an enchanted land, yet it is beset with many perennial concerns including political, immigration, and cultural issues along with the relations with Northern Island.

At the start of the 21st century, due to its diverse export-driven economy, long-term economic issues that best the country were abating. However, the occurrence of a calamity in 2008 brought Ireland's economic crisis.

Largely depending on agriculture, Ireland was long among the poorest regions in Europe with a principal cause of mass migration especially during the 19th-century cycle of famine. More than 40 million Americans were able to trace their ancestry back to Ireland as a result of this exodus. There are millions other people throughout the world who shared the same situation.

Ireland's capital is Dublin, an affluent city which is home to more than 25% of the country's population. Where there were old dockside neighborhoods before, now, new residential and commercial developments take over.

Ireland is divided into four provinces that are further divided into 32 counties. The provinces are:

- Munster
- Leinster
- Ulster
- Connaught

Counties of Munster

- Clare
- Cork
- Kerry
- Limerick
- Tipperary
- Waterford

Counties of Leinster

- Carlow
- Dublin
- Kildare
- Kilkenny
- Laois
- Longford
- Louth
- Meath
- Offaly
- Westmeath
- Wexford
- Wicklow

Counties of Ulster

- Armagh
- Antrim
- Down
- Derry
- Fermanagh
- Tyrone
- Donegal
- Cavan
- Monagham

Counties of Connaught

- Galway
- Leitrim
- Mayo
- Roscommon
- Sligo

The Currency

Throughout the 26 counties of the South, Ireland uses the Euro currency while 6 counties in Ulster use British Pound or Sterling including:

- Down
- Derry
- Antrim
- Armagh
- Tyrone
- Fermanagh

Ireland discontinued the use of Irish Pound, known as "punt" in Gaelic when the country joined the Eurozone.

Climate

The weather in Ireland is largely influenced by the Atlantic Ocean - wet, mild, and changeable. Normal weather condition is not too hot or too cold. It seldom occurs that the summer temperature would go beyond 30 degrees Celsius or 86 degrees Fahrenheit. This can happen once or twice in a decade.

Rainfall can occur anytime in Ireland but a prolonged period of rain is not common, and severe frost and snow are confined to months of December to February.

The Language

Ireland's recognized first official language is Irish Gaelic. However, more than one out of 10 Irish speak a language other than Irish or English. Fingal in Dublin has the highest numbers of non-native languages speakers in the country including Polish, French, and Lithuanian which the most commonly used language in the state.

According to the 2011 census, a total of 182 different languages were recorded to have been spoken across the State.

French is the most common first language used by about 56,430 people nationwide followed by those whose mother tongue is Lithuanian.

Other languages used are the following:

- German
- Russian
- Chinese
- Spanish
- Romanian,
- Latvian

- Arabic
- Portuguese

Lesser-known languages include:

- Shona - the principal language of Zimbabwe (a Niger-Congo language)
- Akan - principally used in Ghana and Ivory Coast

The use of foreign languages is seen as a threat to some people, and if the government will not do something to encourage the use of foreign language, there is a great possibility that these languages will disappear in the coming generations.

Culture and Tradition

The Irish tradition and culture are well known across the globe, and though many are celebrating and enjoying these traditions, still, many don't like their origins.

Here are some of the famous traditions that have helped shaped Irish cultural identity.

Saint Patrick's Day

Patricius was born in a Roman-occupied part of Britain and when she was still 16 years old; she was kidnapped by Irish bandits and sold into slavery as a shepherd. Every day, Patrick prayed to God and each day he believes that God will hear his prayers. After 6 years, he heard God call him to a port which was a hundred miles away from where he was that time. He decided to leave Ireland.

After some time, Patrick saw a vision of lost Irish children, and this convinced him to bring Christianity to Ireland, so he went back. He was famous for comparing the Holy Trinity to Shamrock which then became a famous icon forever linked to Ireland.

After living a long life preaching the Word of Christ, he died on March 17 451 A.D. When the Irish migrated to America in the 19th century; they celebrated St. Patrick's Day and from there, this even became famous and celebrated worldwide.

Pub Culture

In Ireland, the pub culture was integral to the people's daily lives as friends and families are commonly seen in pub houses where they meet and catch up on each other's lives. One of the famous icons that are featured in most pubs is the Guinness. Guinness is a popular alcoholic drink in Ireland and well-known in the world bringing in more than two million euro annually.

Brigid's Cross

Catholicism has been an important element in the history of Ireland, and one image that is being connected to it is the St. Brigid's cross. The image of the cross is made from wild reeds which were said to be created by St. Brigid while trying to convert a dying chieftain into Christianity to convey the story of Jesus Christ crucifixion.

Saint Brigid's day is celebrated every 1st of February which is also the first day of spring in ancient Ireland. Along with the image and the celebration of the event is the belief that the cross would protect your home from fire. This belief continues till the modern time in Ireland.

Halloween

Halloween is a day for trick or treats, and it provides thrills and scares across the world especially to children. However, only a few know that the event originates from the pre-Christian festival "Samhain," where the boundaries between the mortal and the other world would collapse and allow the dead to return to Ireland.

Some people would dress up in a scary costume to ward off bad spirits and would visit homes collecting food for offering to gods. Today, children have innovated this to trick or treat. Offerings are then placed in front of the Tlachta bonfire, and the tradition of great lighting bonfires still continues up to this time.

As part of the celebration, the Gaels carve faces into turnips and made into lanterns to protect themselves from the living dead. Now, these turnips have become pumpkins and are called Jack-O-lanterns.

This tradition originated from the tale about Stingy Jack, a blacksmith who was able to trap the devil using a cross, keeping him as a prisoner. To get out of there, the devil swore to Jack that he wouldn't take Jack's soul after his death. But when Jack died, he was not allowed to enter Heaven, and since the devil keeps up to his promise that he won't take Jack's soul, he was left wandering on earth with only a flame taken from the pit of Hell to light him through the darkness. Jack then place this flame that is never extinguished into a turnip, and that's how it came to be known as the Jack of the Lantern or Jack-O-Lantern. [20]

Irish Music

Pubs hosting live music throughout Ireland prove that music plays an integral part in the Irish culture. Traditional music makes use of world-known music instruments including acoustic guitar, fiddle, and piano combined with local instruments of the Irish natives such as Uilleann pipes, the Celtic harp, and Irish bouzoukis.

There are other Irish traditional instruments apart from the harp that was recently developed like the accordions, the bodhran, concertinas, and the Uilleann pipes emerging only in the 19th century. The guitar and the bouzouki are just off-shoots of the revival of the Irish traditional music in the middle of the 20th century. [21]

Music has taken a large part of Irish existence since prehistoric times.

Even though in the early medieval times, the church contributed greatly to the musical evolution in Ireland. The monastic settlements in Ireland, as well as the rest of Europe, produced what is now known as the *Gregorian chant*. In the secular establishments, musical genres in early Gaelic Ireland can be referred to as a triad of laughing music or *geantraige*, weeping music or *goltraige*, and sleeping music or *suantraige*. Vocal and instrumental music were passed orally back then. The Irish harp holds so much significance that it was declared as Ireland's national symbol.

As for the classical Irish music, it had followed European models as well and was first developed in urban areas and premises where the Anglo-Irish dominated (i.e., Christ Church, Dublin Castle, St. Patrick's Cathedral, and the residences of those with Anglo-Irish roots). Handel's Messiah (1742) became one of the most popular music of the baroque era. In the 19th century, public concerts include classical music to cater to all social classes. Unfortunately, Ireland wasn't generous enough to provide a living to Irish musicians, so the names of the more popular Irish composers of this period belong mostly to emigrants.

The Irish traditional music and dance became globally known in the 1960s. In the mid-twentieth century, Ireland began with its modernization and music was part of this new revolution. Traditional music fell out of favor, particularly in urban areas. However, during the 1960s, the revival of traditional Irish music was led by popular groups like the Clancy Brothers, The Dubliners, The Wolfe Tones, The Chieftains, and Sweeney's Men. Individuals like Christy Moore and Seán Ó Riada also contributed to this revival. Meanwhile, other groups and musicians like Thin Lizzy, Horslips, and Van Morrison combined the elements of Irish traditional music into the contemporary rock during the 1970s and 1980s. This style has become the mainstream nowadays as seen in the works of contemporary artists like The Corrs, Enya, The Cranberries, and many others.

Irish dance, on the other hand, has become famous worldwide in the 1990s with the introduction of Riverdance. Irish dance takes various forms including step dancing, jigs, ceili dances, and reels. It also requires unique fashion sense, with the costumes fashioned based on the designs drawn in the Book of Kells. Although the famed hard shoes that produce clicking sounds during the dance movements were crafted in the nineteenth century. Nowadays, these shoes are commonly made with fiberglass. [22]

Irish Notable Figures

Irish people are famous for their eloquence. Ireland has birthed to a large number of world-class artists, writers, musicians, and politicians.

Michael Collins (1890-1922)

Michael Collins was an Irish revolutionary, soldier, and politician who became a major figure in the early twentieth century during the Irish struggle for independence. He was the *Chairman of the Provisional Government of the Irish Free State* from January 1922 until his death in August 1922.

Collins was initially a member of London GAA and became associated with the *Irish Republican Brotherhood (IRB)* and the *Gaelic League*. He fought in the Easter Rising and was consequently imprisoned in the Frongoch internment camp as one of the prisoners of war. He was released in December 1916 and rose through the ranks in *Sinn Féin* and *Irish Volunteers*.

During the War of Independence, he became the *Director of Organization* and *Adjutant General* for the Irish Volunteers and *Director of Intelligence* of the Irish Republican Army. He also earned the fame as a guerilla warfare strategist due to his skills in planning and commanding many successful attacks on the opponents like the assassination of key British intelligence agents in November 1920.

In 1922 he formed a provisional government and became its chairman but was soon interrupted by the Irish Civil War in which Collins was commander-in-chief of the National Army. Sadly, he was shot and killed during an ambush of anti-Treaty forces on August 22, 1922.

Charles Stewart Parnell (1846-1891)

An Irish nationalist politician, he served as a Member of Parliament (MP) in the *House of Commons of the United Kingdom of Great Britain and Ireland* from 1875 to 1880. He was born into an influential Anglo-Irish Protestant family, became a land reform activist, and the founder of the *Irish National Land League* in 1879. He was famous for his skills in executing parliamentary procedures and in stabilizing radical, economic, and constitutional issues. Parnell is greatly admired as the best political party organizer of his time and also one of the most intimidating figures in parliamentary history.

Bono (1960- Present)

Paul David Hewson or Bono is an Irish singer, musician, songwriter, businessman, and philanthropist. He is best known as the lead vocalist and main lyricist of the rock band U2. His lyrics bring social, political and spiritual awareness. As a U2 member, Bono has bagged 22 Grammy Awards and have been inducted into the Rock and Roll Hall of Fame.

Outside his profession as a musician, Bono is famous for his activism for social justice causes, being active in his campaigns for Africa, and for which he co-founded the ONE Campaign, DATA, and EDUN. Due to his humanitarian contributions, he was given an honorary knighthood by Queen Elizabeth II. Bono was also named as one of the Time Persons of the Year in 2005.

Aside from the icons mentioned above, these famous individuals greatly contributed to the name of their country and respective fields:

- Samuel Beckett (playwright, Nobel Prize awardee)
- George Bernard Shaw (playwright, Nobel Prize awardee)
- William Butler Yeats (poet, Nobel Prize awardee)
- Robert Boyle (chemist, physicist)
- John Philip Holland (inventor)
- William Edward Wilson (astronomer)
- John Tyndall (physicist)
- Oscar Wilde (poet and dramatist)
- Brendan Behan (satirist, poet, and playwright)
- Jonathan Swift (satirist and essayist)
- James Joyce (novelist)
- Sean O'Casey (playwright)
- Edmund Burke (political theorist)
- Pierce Brosnan (actor)
- Collin Farrell (actor)
- Ronan Keating (singer)
- Westlife (band)

Potatoes

Potato isn't just a food staple in Ireland but also a popular symbol. The potato obtained its importance as a crop in Ireland right before the famine. It was not a native Irish crop but had been found by Spanish in South America in the 1500s and was shipped to Europe, reaching Ireland at around 1590.

The farmers realized eventually that potatoes could double the food and everyone would have enough to eat. They could also still have land to grow oats and get involved in dairying at the same time. The plant allowed the farmers to make extra money. Eventually, potatoes were also planted in Connaught and Leinster, even becoming the staple food for the farm laborers. The lands in the east were converted into tillage farms while the Ulster was used to grow flax for the Irish linen industry. That time, Dublin was progressing as an urban center. These factors helped the potato economy surge, and soon farmers were selling their excess crops to the regions where food are scarce. Also, new potato varieties like Apple Potato (1760), Cup Potato (1800), and Lumper Potato (after 1810) were introduced. Potatoes became a primary source of nutrition for the poorest people of Leinster and Connaught.

In the early 1800s, the population was boosted to over 8 million that many of the farmers and their laborers became almost reliant on potatoes. By 1830s, about thirty to thirty-five percent of the Irish had potatoes as their staple food. Fortunately, potatoes are excellent in nutrition. If milk is added, it can provide enough protein, minerals, carbohydrates, and energy needed for a balanced diet.

In 1700, a Connaught farmer could have eaten one meal with potatoes per day; in 1800, the number doubled. As the potato spread, farmers had little ability to acquire oats and milk. By 1840, a Connaught farmer was eating three potato meals per day, containing a total of five to six kilograms of potatoes.

On the eve of the Great Famine, a third of the Irish population in Connaught and Munster relied on potatoes as their main food source. Since potatoes could not be stored for a long time or transported well, a new crop needed to be grown per year. [22]

Irish Legends and Folklores

When it comes to literary treasures, Ireland proves to be one of the richest in Western Europe. Even the individual characters like the Banshee, leprechaun, and changeling have become world-renowned.

The Banshee, one of the most popular in the lot, is derived from the Irish *bean-sidhe* which means a woman of the fairy. It's an ancestral spirit that warms families of approaching tragedies like personal losses and death. According to legends, she can only warn the five prestigious families: the O'Conners, O'Neils, O'Gradys, O'Byrons, and Kavanaghs. Thus, she's also a spirit symbolizing prestige and affluence. Appearing before the family members (or hearing her wails) portends death. She is also known to accompany the dead to the afterlife.

Her appearance can be that of a young woman, a middle-aged lady, or an old hag. In some stories, the banshee is said to take other forms like the stoat, weasel, crow, and other animals familiar to witches. King James I of Scotland was rumored to have been confronted by a banshee shortly before his demise.

Some Irish myths can also be seen in the history of other places like the Tales of the Irish hunter-warrior, Fionn Mac Cumhaill and his conflict with a Scottish giant named Benandonner. In order to avoid getting his feet wet, he created the Giant's Causeway. To scare the opposition, he threw a mass of land into the direction of Scotland but missed. The mass landed in the Irish Sea and came to be what is known now as the Isle of Man; the pebble of the projectile forming Rockall; the hole from where he scooped the land was filled with water and became Lough Neagh. Related tales of this legend were also told in the Scottish and Manx folktales.

Perhaps the most popular character among the Irish legends and folklore is the gold-obsessed leprechaun, a fairy of the Tuath Dé Danann known to be a supernatural tribe of gods from the Otherworld and who also ruled as deities of Ireland. The pint-sized fairies are portrayed as mischievous cobblers who own great wealth and grant three wishes to any human who captures them. Originally, leprechauns were known to dress in red jackets instead of green. [23]

Irish Literature and Theater

Irish literature has great influence all over the world, and a big part of its soul is from the Irish cultural identity. Their rich collection of mythology was preserved by the monks during medieval times. They were written both in Latin and the Old Irish language. The Normans introduced the English writing in Ireland during the thirteenth century. By the nineteenth century, the Irish literature was mainly written in English.

Ireland has produced great writers including Jonathan Swift, author of Gulliver's Travels, and the first world-renowned Irish writer. Oscar Wilde, the humorous and controversial playwright and author of The Picture of Dorian Gray. Dracula was written by the very much Irish Bram Stoker and the children's favorite, The Chronicles of Narnia, was written by C.S. Lewis.

Aside from Oscar Wilde, Ireland also gave birth to successful playwrights like Samuel Beckett and George Bernard Shaw. Geniuses like Seamus Heaney, W.B. Yeats, and Patrick Kavanagh greatly contributed to the field of poetry. There are also those whose writing skills have been conveyed in both Gaelic and English languages like Flann O'Brien and Brendan Behan.

In the 1920s, the Irish literature was internationally prominent with the modernist authors like James Joyce accomplishing popularity with *A Portrait of the Artist as a Young Man* and *Dubliners*, and notoriety with his novels, *Finnegans Wake* and *Ulysses*. In the 21st century, Colum McCann and Roddy Doyle along with the female writers such as Emma Donoghue, Jennifer Johnston, and Ann Enright contributed to the steady popularity of the Irish writing. Irish literature is continuously experiencing revival, always claiming its place in the global literary world. [24]

Conclusion

What seemed to be an unending struggle of political and religious power in Ireland had long been over, but the memory that it left behind will remain a lesson especially to the common people who bore all the consequences.

The English have long pulled out their armies and commanders, but the thousands of lives that were sacrificed will never be regained back.

But what lesson have we learned from the past?

Until recently, Irish history tells how the Irish resisted and finally overcame the oppressive dominance of the English rule and its collaborators. However, lately, this was questioned by a new generation of Irish historians leading to a deeper understanding of the past and drawing a different conclusion and lesson from it.

Let us consider the famous Irish Potato Famine in 1840. In 1845, there was an infestation of a fungal parasite – Phytophthora infestans resulting in a partial failure of the harvest of Irish potato that year. Also because of wet weather, there was again another harvest failure in 1847 and 1848 which resulted in the death of more than one and a half million people who died from hunger and famine-related sickness. To avoid the calamity, an equal number of Irish migrated to other countries including the United States of America. Due to this and to subsequent mass migration, Ireland has failed to recover demographically. In 1841 the population of Ireland is 8 million and today, there are only 6 million.

Although the British had their fair share of the blame for the great disaster, notice that the unending conflicts between religious sectors played a dominant role in what happened to the Irish. When at first there was this power play between the King and the Pope, later it became Catholicism vs. Protestantism. The irony here is the fact that both parties employ violence and politics to get what they want. Instead of leading the people in the right way, their misdeed led to the death of many.

When Penal Laws were passed and used as instruments for curtailing the rights of the Catholics, including foreboding them to go overseas for education, and for teaching or operating schools, nonetheless, what created a great impact was the Act to Prevent the Further Growth of Popery which prevented Catholics from buying lands or inheriting it from Protestants and from leasing lands beyond the period of 31 years.

When at this time, potatoes were considered a major crop, the existing legislature and penal laws were enough to discourage the farmers from planting crops and improving their agricultural practice. With the set-up advantageous only to the landlords who were Protestants, the Catholic farmers were never motivated to develop their lands for farming.

While Irish agriculture remained to be labor-intensive and the land repeatedly subdivided, a family survived in a small area because of the high yield of potato. However, these restraints on the majority also meant that the commerce and national gross production of Ireland are not developing resulting in low economic status. Added to this was the migration of many Irish to other places which had a great impact on its demographics.

Therefore, it is easy to see that that the root of the problem was actually the nature of the land system. With a policy that allows landowners to keep a large area of lands and yet prevents agricultural improvements is bound to keep the national economy is a disastrous state.

Furthermore, there was this Corn Law preventing large-scale importation of grains into Ireland which further aggravates the food shortage until it was repealed in 1846.

From the history of Ireland, we can learn that not all governments are effective in relieving disasters. In fact, some even aggravate the situation because of the political power plays which in this case is even magnified with the violent participation of religious sectors.

Another thing is laws that affect economic choices can have long-term and frequently perverse results. In the case of Ireland, actions and laws that led to wrong economic incentives produce effects that are difficult to reverse.

Finally, if you found this book useful in any way, a review is always appreciated!

BIBLIOGRAPHY

[16] Adventurers' Act. (2007, April 19). Retrieved from
    https://en.wikipedia.org/wiki/Adventurers_Act

[3] A Brief History of Ireland. (n.d.). Retrieved from
    http://www.localhistories.org/irehist.html

[4] Celtic Ireland in the Iron Age: the Celts. (n.d.). Retrieved from
    http://www.wesleyjohnston.com/users/ireland/past/pre_norma
    n_history/iron_age.html

[17] Confederate Ireland. (n.d.). Retrieved from
    https://en.wikipedia.org/wiki/Confederate_Ireland

[19] Connacht. (2002, August 21). Retrieved from
    https://en.wikipedia.org/wiki/Connacht

[10] Edward VI of England. (2001, December 11). Retrieved from
    https://en.wikipedia.org/wiki/Edward_VI_of_England

[20] History - Modern Ireland. (n.d.). Retrieved from
    http://www.ireland-information.com/reference/modirel.html

[14] History of Ireland 1598 - 1629: Defeat of Ulster and the Ulster
    Plantation. (n.d.). Retrieved from
    http://www.wesleyjohnston.com/users/ireland/past/history/15
    981629.html

[9] Holy See. (2001, May 4). Retrieved from
    https://en.wikipedia.org/wiki/Holy_See

Ireland in the Age of the Tudors. (n.d.). Retrieved from
    http://www.askaboutireland.ie/learning-zone/primary-
    students/subjects/history/history-the-full-story/ireland-in-the-
    age-of-the/

[1] Ireland in the last Ice Age. (n.d.). Retrieved from
    http://www.wesleyjohnston.com/users/ireland/past/pre_norma
    n_history/iceage.html

[Ireland. (n.d.). Retrieved from
    https://en.wikipedia.org/wiki/Ireland#Arts

[13] Irish Rebellion of 1641. (2005, February 2). Retrieved from

https://en.wikipedia.org/wiki/Irish_Rebellion_of_1641

[5] John's first expedition to Ireland. (2004, November 4). Retrieved from
https://en.wikipedia.org/wiki/John%27s_first_expedition_to_I
reland

[12] Mary I of England. (n.d.). Retrieved from
https://en.wikipedia.org/wiki/Mary_I_of_England

[2] Neolithic Stone Age in Prehistoric Ireland. (n.d.). Retrieved from
http://www.wesleyjohnston.com/users/ireland/past/pre_norma
n_history/neolithic_age.html

[22] Prelude to the Irish Famine: The Potato. (n.d.). Retrieved from
https://www.wesleyjohnston.com/users/ireland/past/famine/p
otato.html

[13] Second Desmond Rebellion. (2006, July 21). Retrieved from
https://en.wikipedia.org/wiki/Second_Desmond_Rebellion#S
econd_rebellion

[22]Ten Irish Cultural Traditions and Their Origins. (2018,
September 14). Retrieved from
https://www.irelandbeforeyoudie.com/ten-origins-irish-
cultural-traditions/

[23] Top 10 Irish Mythological Creatures | Irish Folklore. (2017,
September 11). Retrieved from http://blog.carrolls.ie/top-10-
irish-mythological-creatures/

[2] Vikings in Ireland. (n.d.). Retrieved March 19, 2019, from
http://www.wesleyjohnston.com/users/ireland/past/pre_norma
n_history/vikings.html

[16] West Indies. (2002, January 27). Retrieved from
https://en.wikipedia.org/wiki/West_Indies

CPSIA information can be obtained
at www.ICGtesting.com
Printed in the USA
FSHW020501180621
82500FS